Between Anxiety and Hope

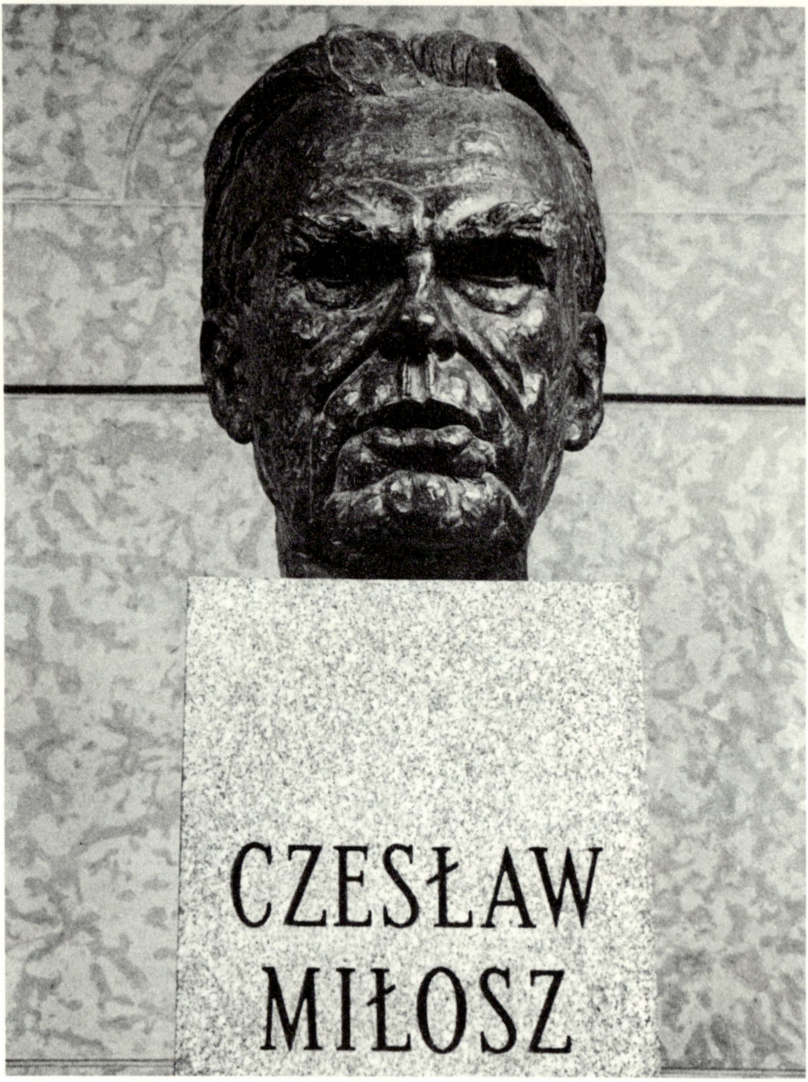

Bust of Czesław Miłosz by Edmonton artist Danek Możdżeński. A gift of the Polish Cultural Society to the University of Alberta, it was unveiled on March 22, 1984 and is on permanent display at the Rutherford Library South, University of Alberta, Edmonton, Alberta.

BETWEEN ANXIETY AND HOPE

The Poetry and Writing of CZESŁAW MIŁOSZ

EDITED BY
Edward Możejko

THE UNIVERSITY OF ALBERTA PRESS

First published by
The University of Alberta Press
Athabasca Hall
Edmonton, Alberta, Canada
1988

ISBN 0-88864-127-3

Canadian Cataloguing in Publication Data

Main entry under title:
Between anxiety and hope

ISBN 0-88864-127-3
1. Miłosz, Czesław - Criticism and interpretation. I. Możejko, Edward.
PG7158.M5532B48 1988 891.8'517 C87-091272-0

Typesetting by Typeworks, Vancouver, British Columbia, Canada
Printed by John Deyell Company, Lindsay, Ontario, Canada

CONTENTS

ABBREVIATIONS

The following abbreviations have been used to cite quotations of Czesław Miłosz's poetry and prose in the text:

MIŁOSZ'S BOOKS

BW	*Bells in Winter*
CP	*The Collected Poems, 1931–1987*
GWS	*Gdzie wschodzi słońce i kędy zapada*
GZ	*Gucio zaczarowany*
IV	*The Issa Valley*
MBI	*Miasto bez imienia*
NR	*Native Realm*
O	*Ocalenie*
PIII	*Poezje*, Vol. III
RE	*Rodzinna Europa*
SD	*Światło dzienne*
SN	*The Separate Notebooks*
SP	*Selected Poems*
TP	*Traktat Poetycki*
TZ	*Trzy zimy. Poezje*
UP	*Utwory poetyckie. Poems*
VSF	*Visions from San Francisco Bay*
W(1967)	*Wiersze (1967)*
WP	*The Witness of Poetry*
WSF	*Widzenia nad zatoką San Francisco*
ZU	*Ziemia Ulro*

Other Sources

WLT	*World Literature Today* 52, no. 3 (Summer 1978)

Complete bibliographic information can be found in the "List of Czesław Miłosz's Books" and the "Selected Bibliography" at the end of this book.

Translations by the individual contributors are initialed.

tr. B.C.	translated by Bogdan Czaykowski
tr. P.C.	translated by Paul Coates
tr. M.L.	translated by Madeline G. Levine
tr. E.M.	translated by Edward Możejko
tr. A.R.	translated by Allan Reid

PREFACE

In the recent history of twentieth century Polish literature, Czesław Miłosz occupies a unique position: he is the first Polish poet to be awarded the Nobel Prize for literature. His two other countrymen who attained the same distinction were novelists: Henryk Sienkiewicz was honoured with the Nobel Prize in 1905 (incidentally, he was the first Slavic author ever to receive such a mark of preference) and Władysław S. Reymont in 1924 for his "roman fleuve" *Chłopi* (The Peasants). Considering the belated emergence of Polish prose on the national, and even more so, on the international literary scene, this succinct juxtaposition of facts runs contrary to the logic of literary evolution in Poland and suggests a paradox. For if, indeed, we are to ask the question of what constitutes the main generic canon of Polish literature, the answer must be unequivocal: it is poetry. Its national tradition can be traced from as far back as the Renaissance poetry of J. Kochanowski and the sonnets of M. Sęp-Szarzyński, through the Latin odes of M.K. Sarbiewski and the Baroque lyrics of the Morsztyn brothers to nineteenth century Romanticism with its most prominent representatives —A Mickiewicz, J. Słowacki, Z. Krasiński and C.K. Norwid. It is exactly this tradition that brought the literature of Poland into the broader realm of European culture.

In view of such an evolution, the legitimacy of which can be hardly questioned, the distinction bestowed on Czesław Miłosz seems to carry a particular weight and as such deserves a closer examination. Realizing the significance of Miłosz's poetry, it should be also noted that this collection of essays is not an empty glorification—on the contrary, it is composed of a series of analytical, in some instances even polemical statements which in acknowledging Miłosz's prominence try to give a balanced assessment of his creative literary output. At the same time, this book is a tribute to a poet who managed not only to continue to develop the rich tradition of a national poetry, but also to raise and respond to some fundamental questions of our epoch, to move hearts and feelings wherever his poetic word reached an audience.

Whence stems Czesław Miłosz's unusual power to touch the reader's sensitivity? The question is too complex to be answered in brief, but some general lines along which one can attempt an explanation clearly emerge. Miłosz, from the very beginning of his poetic journey, denounced the concept of poetry as a formal experiment which dazzles with its endless gimmickry of literary devices. On the contrary, poetry is an intricate relationship between the poet and the outer world. It grows out of the intimate experience which the poet, as medium, accumulates throughout his life. Despite his painful awareness of both linguistic and generic limitations of poetry as a means of individual expression or communication, the poet has no right to rescind his moral responsibility towards his fellow contemporaries. Hence, the urge to sensitize them to some horrific questions which preoccupy his own mind and poetic imagination. In advancing such a concept of poetry, Miłosz took a tremendous gamble. It was indeed a gamble, because he was clearly moving against the mainstream of literary tendencies (e.g., avant-garde, the onslaught of post-modernism and socialist-realist propaganda literature); he risked being outplayed by his own time or labelled an outmoded epigon. Yet Miłosz, it seems, did not mind challenging the pitfalls which ephemeral fashions tend to create. Although his poetry raised some essential, if not existential questions of our time, Miłosz again and again objected to the label of a modernist or avant-gardist poet, attributed to him by some critics. Indeed, Miłosz has detested classifications and distrusted labels as few others have.

The paradox of being considered a modernist (I use the word in the sense ascribed to it by Anglo-Saxon critical tradition) on the one hand, and rejecting this idea on the other, explains, I believe, the very essence, specificity and greatness of Miłosz's poetry. Qualifiers such as "modernist" or "avant-gardist" are too closely associated with sterile experimentation and have nothing to do with the main thrust of his writing which aims at conveying a message rather than only demonstrating linguistic dexterity or virtuosity. In fact, at the centre of Miłosz's aesthetics stands the reader. Yet it would be erroneous to claim that Miłosz's poetry is devoid of any experiment; innovation remains an important constituent of his poetry. What we ought to realize, however, is the poet's innovative devices always contain a strong component of expediency. It rests on what Wallace Stevens called "the commonplace," which generates serious reflection without using comic or tragic expressive modes. Miłosz's poems strike us with their narrativity or narrative tone, the simplicity of which both captivates and deceives; it deceives because it contains ambiguity which often borders on the proverbial. In short, it finds its origins in the literature of wisdom.

Few writers of modern literature have displayed the same great sense of historicity and susceptibility to the problems of contemporaneity as has Miłosz. Although he was praised and initially gained recognition in the West thanks to his exposure of the dangers of totalitarian systems, and of communism in particular, the strength and significance of his writing can hardly be limited to, or explained by this theme alone. Albeit significant, it constitutes only a part of the extraordinarily broad range of questions which tell about the global crisis of our civilization. In such conditions the act of writing cannot be a game, but an act of personal courage through which the poet makes a heroic effort to take exception to the world which has lost its primordial innocence. It is an act of meaningful disapproval built upon such opposites as condemnation and love, despair and hope. These opposites, however, grow out of a more encompassing, central conflict between historicity and the search for some transcendental ethical values which can defy the reign of relativity and decay of human values on a global scale. The importance of historicity in Miłosz cannot be overemphasized. A clear sense of historicity prompts his opposition to and discord with (to paraphrase the existential expression) *condition inhumaine* of our time. Hence both the meditative and visionary character of his poetry.

The idea of publishing this collection of articles on Czesław Miłosz emerged slowly from certain developments which occurred both among a few staff members at the University of Alberta and the Polish community in Edmonton. In this sense, these articles constitute an excellent exemplification of fruitful cooperation between the University and its social, cultural environment. Indeed, it is a living manifestation of something that should be particularly cherished in our time, that is, direct contact between the humanities, as practised by scholars interested in important literary issues, and on the other hand, laymen, who support such initiatives and by the same token wish to make a contribution to the revival of a deteriorating discipline. Although the factors which spurred the project are of local significance, they created a favourable ambience for pursuing the publication of this collection. It should be emphasized, however, that the true motivation behind the whole initiative is different: it reveals a great fascination with the phenomenon called Czesław Miłosz.

When the Swedish Academy awarded Czesław Miłosz the Nobel Prize for Literature in 1980, he was not an unknown literary personality in Edmonton. Even before that date, a number of people here considered him to be an outstanding writer and tried to attract the attention of readers to his poetry and prose. I regularly included a discussion of Miłosz's works as part of my lectures on Polish literature at the University of Alberta and in the late sixties recommended to the Polish library (owned by the Polish community) the purchase of Miłosz's books because "one day he will win the Nobel Prize for literature." Frankly, it was a naive reason to use, and I did not realize how "prophetic" these words were to be, but at that time it was, at least in some cases, a good way to catch the attention of quite a few people and to indicate to them the magnitude of Miłosz's creative genius.

Thanks to the initiative of such people as Professors Leszek and Marytka Kosiński, Professor Aleksander Matejko and Mrs. Joanna Matejko, Miłosz was invited to Edmonton for the first time in February 1972. The second visit took place at the invitation of Professor Karol Krótki, the president of the Polish Cultural Society, which in cooperation with the University of Alberta, organized in September of 1981 the so-called "Miłosz Days in Edmonton." The thought of editing a book on Miłosz crystallized at that time. Originally, it was intended that the papers, which were presented at the symposium during "Miłosz Days in Edmonton," would be published. Unfortunately, the project remained dormant for some time, but did not die. In the beginning of 1984, the Canadian Polish Congress (Alberta Branch) decided to patronize the project and take control of its financing. In the meantime, those authors who originally intended to participate reworked their papers, and some others expressed interest in joining the project. Among these were Professor Stanisław Bereś of Wrocław University, a prominent authority on the so-called "second avant-garde" (his Ph.D. was titled "Poezja Żagarystów 1931–1945") and author of numerous articles on Miłosz; E.D. Blodgett, professor of Comparative Literature and a poet himself; and Professor Paul Coates, author of the recently published book *Words After Speech* (1986) which makes a significant contribution to the comparative study of European Romanticism and Symbolism.

From its inception, the prime purpose of this book was to analyze *various aspects* of Miłosz writings. Consequently, no leading theme was presupposed or imposed. In retrospect, it could be said that a few of the essays and articles included in this volume are permeated with discussion of the concept of reality in Miłosz's poetry. Understandably, another topic dominates observations on Miłosz too: catastrophism, which constitutes one of the major motifs of his poetry. Here the readers will also find an analysis of Miłosz's political prose, his place in Polish literature and dialectical entanglements which besiege his poetic "I." In one article, Miłosz's poetic conceptions, as developed in *The Witness of Poetry*, are juxtaposed with the artistic attitudes of some Canadian poets.

The book also includes an appendix which provides brief information about Miłosz's visits to Canada. The reason for this inclusion deserves an explanation. Miłosz, as no other Nobel Prize laureate, travelled to this country frequently (often at the invitation and encouragement of the Polish Canadians) and established lasting ties with intellectual and literary circles on the northern side of the world's longest border. It should suffice to mention that the best translator of Miłosz's artistic prose, Professor L. Iribarne, resides in Toronto. Those who admire Miłosz are thankful to the poet for the opportunities his visits created to experience the magic power of his poetry. This fact should not go unnoticed. To be sure, the appendix does not detail the complete itineraries of the poet's visits to Canada. Still, in our opinion, it may become an important source of information and provide valuable clues to those who may wish to search for material on Miłosz's life and poetry. Thus it supplements the major objective of this collection, the analysis of various aspects of Miłosz's writing, with a factual background which in this case shows Miłosz's ties with Canada.

ACKNOWLEDGMENTS

First of all I would like to express my sincere appreciation to Czesław Miłosz himself. In correspondence with me, he kindly gave his consent to quote excerpts from his works and helped to translate those poems which, so far, had not been available in English. It was, indeed, wonderful to feel Professor Miłosz's personal interest and assistance in solving some difficult editorial matters relating to the translations. He expressed doubt to me whether some of his poems were translatable, mentioning twice that "Kołysanka" ("Lullaby") was "nieprzetłumaczalna"—"untranslatable." It also surprised him, and perhaps slightly irritated him, to find that some of his early poems which he never included in any of his collections have been quoted by Dr. Bereś in his article. Professor Miłosz's cordial and understanding attitude towards my publishing initiative not only had an inspiring and rewarding effect on those participating in the process of editing the manuscript, but also lent it a special dimension and new, quality: this book now contains excerpts and even whole poems which are translated into English for the first time.

The preparation of this volume of articles, sponsored by the Canadian Polish Congress (Alberta Branch) in cooperation with the Department of Comparative Literature, University of Alberta, was made possible thanks to a generous grant from the Alberta Cultural Heritage Foundation and donations from the Polish Canadian Society, Edmonton; the Polish Women's Federation, Branch No. 3, Edmonton; the Polish Combatant's Association, Branch No. 6, Edmonton; the Polish Cultural Society, Edmonton; the Polish Canadian Society, Lethbridge; the Polish Combatant's Association, Lethbridge; the Polish Academic and Businessmen's Club, the Canadian Polish Congress (Alberta Branch); and the Polish Veterans Society, Edmonton. As editor, I would like to express my sincere appreciation to all these organizations and the people who showed genuine interest inthe successful implementation of this project.

Our special thanks go to the secretary of the Department of Slavic and East European Studies, Mrs. Doreen Hawryshko, for her unselfish help, tireless typing and retyping of the manuscript. Without her devotion of many hours towards the preparation of the final version of this manuscript, its completion would have been delayed considerably.

I would also like to pay tribute to the late student Mieczysław Klefter, who helped me in the initial stage of preparing the manuscript for publication. His sudden and untimely death not only slowed the work, but shocked those who knew his enthusiasm for Slavic studies and left his friends with the feeling of irretrievable loss, with an empty corner in their hearts.

After the manuscript was submitted to and accepted for publication by the University of Alberta Press, it went through a thoughtful and intelligent reading by Ms. Mary Mahoney-Robson. Her care and personal commitment to produce a high quality book helped immensely to shape the final version of the text. For an author there cannot be anything more fulfilling and encouraging than a friendly and caring editor. I wish to express my sincere appreciation to Ms. Mahoney-Robson for her tireless and creative assistance.

Cordial thanks go also to my assistant Anita Dorczak who, with great patience and devotion, typed and retyped many times the suggested improvements, meticulously checked references, quotes and compiled the enclosed bibliography. She should also be credited with helping to prepare the index of names, titles, and subjects. As well, the work of three other students in the Department of Comparative Literature, Paul Morris, Weiqun-Dai and Sharon Ryan, is recognized with gratitude. It was Ms. Ryan who was responsible for making up the final version of the index.

Words of thankfulness should be expressed to Mr. Allen Reid and Mr. Laird Taylor for translating Professor Bereś's and my introductory article, respectively. Some of Czesław Miłosz's poems and excerpts, which were only available in Polish, were translated into English by myself. I would like to express my appreciation to Professor Robert Solomon from the Department of English, University of Alberta, for helping me with the translations needed for this book.

The Ecco Press, Miłosz's publisher in New York, has granted permission for quoting excerpts of Miłosz's poems that have been translated previously.

Last but not least, I would like to express my profound gratitude to my wife Sheila for not only a patient proofreading of the texts, but also for her loving support and understanding of my work.

ABOUT THE CONTRIBUTORS

STANISŁAW BEREŚ is Professor of Polish literature at the University of Wrocław, Poland. He wrote his Ph.D. on "Poezja Żagarystów 1931–1945" (The Poetry of Żagarists 1931–1945) and published numerous articles on Czesław Miłosz and other Żagarists poets: "Wokół 'Poematu o czasie zastygłym'," "Rozważania nad programem Żagarów," "Największy poeta miasta Lidy," "Ostatni bard Wielkiego Księstwa," "'Muzyka zodiaków, zjawisk i cyfr,' Poezja Jerzego Zagórskiego do 1933 Roku" and many others.

E.D. BLODGETT is Professor of Canadian and comparative literature in the Department of Comparative Literature, at the University of Alberta. A well-known Canadian poet, his collections of poetry include *Take away the names, Sounding, Beast gate, Arché/elegies*. He is also the author of *Configuration: Essays in the Canadian literatures.*

PAUL COATES graduated in German at Churchill College, Cambridge, where he also studied Polish. He completed his Ph.D. on the Polish Symbolist Bolesław Leśmian at the University of Warsaw. As a critic and translator, his publications include: *The Realist Fantasy: Fiction and Reality Since "Clarissa"* (1983), *The Story of Lost Reflection: The Alienation of the Image in Western and Polish Cinema* (1985), *Identyczność i nieidentyczność w twórczości Bolesława Leśmiana* (1986), *Words After Speech* (1986). He has contributed to various journals such as *PN Review, New Left Review* and the *Comparative Criticism Yearbook.* At present, he is Professor of English at McGill University, Montreal.

BOGDAN CZAYKOWSKI is Professor and Head of the Department of Slavonic Studies, University of British Columbia. A well-known poet of the London *Kontynenty* group, his published collections of poetry include *Trzciny czcionek, Spór z granicami, Point-no-point,* as well as numerous articles on Polish literature, including "Post-war Polish poets" in *The Tradition of Polish Ideals,* edited by W.J. Stankiewicz (1981).

MADELINE G. LEVINE is Professor and Chairman of the Department of Slavic Languages, the University of North Carolina at Chapel Hill. Professor M.G. Levine specializes in Polish and Russian literatures. Her book *Contemporary Polish Poetry* 1925–1975 appeared in 1981.

EDWARD MOŻEJKO is Professor and Chairman of the Department of Comparative Literature, University of Alberta and is a Fellow of the Royal Society of Canada. His books on Slavic and comparative literature include: *Sztuka pisarska Jordana Jowkowa* (1964), *Iwan Wazow* (1967), *Socialist Realism: Theory, Evolution, Decline* (1977), *Vasilij Pavlovich Aksenov: A Writer in Quest of Himself* (1986), editor, together with P. Dalgaard and B. Briker. His publications also include articles on such writers as R. Petrović, M. Krleža, J. Seifert, O. Mandelstam and others.

Between Anxiety and Hope

Czesław Miłosz.

Photo by D. Możdżeński.

EDWARD MOŻEJKO

Between the Universals of Moral Sensibility and Historical Consciousness

Notes on the Writings of Czesław Miłosz

A general synthesis of Czesław Miłosz's works is at present almost impracticable. The difficulty in accomplishing such a general presentation, even the shortest, stems mainly from the fact that we must sketch the silhouette of a writer whose name, although known in creative circles, until recently had little meaning to the general public in Poland or elsewhere and, paradoxically, remained almost unknown to the average reader among the emigrant community. This observation is also confirmed by K. Dybciak in his detailed analysis of Miłosz's reception in his own country and abroad. He notes that the reader, especially in Poland, was taken unawares of Miłosz being awarded the Nobel Prize for literature because "many of his [that is Miłosz's] compatriots heard about his existence for the first time."[1] Despite some improvements, no doubt, the number of essays and articles about Miłosz has steadily grown since 1980, this situation justifies the necessity for an informative, yet cursory, discussion of the outer facts of the writer's biography, the life and poetry of the author combined with an overview of the main ideas and aesthetic principles of his work. However, because such a dazzling wealth of thoughts, of motifs, of philosophical, religious and social themes opens before us, we are not quite sure what to exclude from so great an intellectual output and what to include as containing important information, so as to give as comprehensive and as objective a view as possible of the works of the author of *Zniewolony umysł (The Captive Mind).*

Therefore, my discussion of Miłosz's works does not pretend to exhaust the subject; it is rather intended as an introduction to the questions dealt with in this book and to raise some crucial issues of an authorship permeated from beginning to end with a high-minded *reflective tone.* When speaking of Miłosz's reflectiveness, one can hardly resist the impression that it is tinged with a certain degree of moralizing. As a rule, modern writers detest this sort of qualification but one should not forget that shortly before her death, the eminent and internationally acclaimed Canadian author Margaret Laurence stated in one of her interviews that a great writer cannot avoid being a moralist. And I should add that what I have in mind here is not a simplified understanding of this concept. By this is meant neither a type of Rosary Hour moralizing, nor even the broadly understood attitude towards the world conditioned by the Roman Catholic *Weltanschaung.* In an address given on the occasion of his being granted an honorary doctorate by the Catholic University of Lublin, Miłosz expressed his opposition to views which would qualify him as a Catholic writer. What form of moralizing is meant,[2] then, and what is the essence of its meaning? It seems to spring from a strong desire to sensitize man's conscience to the universal existential problems which are expressed in terms of good and evil, to problems religious, philosophical, national and social alike, which are of concern to those conditioned by a particular historical experience, but equally of concern to individuals living at all latitudes. This moralizing springs from an incessant *anxiety* and from *hope;* its source is the wealth of the Judeo-Christian tradition and the cultural and civilizing experiences of all mankind. Man is not a one-dimensional being, but a tangle of varying experiences. From this belief springs the *polyphonic* nature of Miłosz's poetry and its appeal to the reader.

Czesław Miłosz was born on April 30, 1911 in Szetajnie, Poland, not far from Vilno. His education began in Vilno, and in 1935 he graduated from the Faculty of Law at Stefan Batory University. In 1930 his first poetic works were printed at his alma mater in Vilno. One year later, together with the young poets Jerzy Zagórski, Teodor Bujnicki, Aleksander Rymkiewicz, Jerzy Putrament and Józef Maśliński, Miłosz formed the poetic group *Żagary*,[3] which lasted until 1934 and gave birth to a phenomenon known in the most recent annals of Polish literature as the "second literary avant-garde." Miłosz's first two collections of poetry appeared in the thirties: the first, from the year 1933, was entitled *Poemat o czasie zastygłym* (Poem on Time Frozen); the second was printed in 1936 under the title of *Trzy zimy* (Three Winters). The latter particularly heralded the arrival of a new voice in Polish poetry; it drew the attention of literary critics and won favourable criticism. The early poetry by the author of *Traktat poetycki* (Poetic Treatise) set itself in opposition to the existing aesthetic programs formulated at the eve of Poland's independence in 1918 and practised throughout the twenties by the Warsaw group *Skamander*, whose members included J. Tuwim, A. Słonimski, J. Lechoń, J. Iwaszkiewicz, K. Wierzyński. It also opposed the programs of the Cracovian avant-garde[4] represented by such poets as T. Peiper, J. Przyboś, J. Brzękowski and J. Kurek. Miłosz not only broke with their impulsive biologism and often superficial social commitment; he also rejected the decidedly exaggerated, incomprehensible use of metaphors by the Cracovian avant-garde, their technocratism, their fascination with industrial progress as expressed in the slogan, "The City, The Masses, The Machine." In the camp of the Vilno poets (Żagarists), the conviction reigned that the Cracovian avant-garde's hermetic use of metaphors often concealed a lack of substance and a mental void. This is not the place to discuss the differences separating the various poetic groupings. It is sufficient to mention that in the discovery of new aesthetic approaches, in the breaking-down of existing poetic conventions, in the formulation of new poetics, and in the determination of a new role for poetry, Czesław Miłosz played a decisive part—he opened to contemporary sensibilities hitherto unknown areas of experience and perceptions of reality.

The singularity of Miłosz's poetic pronouncement was classified by literary critics as belonging to the "second avant-garde"; its early phase was defined as *catastrophism*. This latter aspect of Miłosz's poetry defines the aforementioned peculiarity most distinctly. What does this concept convey? On the whole, it expresses pessimism and the endangerment of mankind in the contemporary world. The poet desires to warn humanity; or to make it aware of the existence of some undefined danger of cataclysm, to jolt the conscience of man through the placement of his existence in some alien, uncertain world drifting towards catastrophe. Miłosz's early poetry, written before 1939, is in great measure pervaded by an apocalyptic vision which at times assumes a form of ironic alternation of pastoral, idyllic descriptions of reality with a mournful spectre of war or general calamity. This is clearly visible in the poem "Kołysanka" ("Lullaby"):

Nad filarami, z których smoła ścieka,
w prowincji tej, gdzie salwa codzień błyska,
pod śpiew saperów o losie człowieka
kołysze płacz dziecinny kołyska.

Kołysze, lula nowego bohatera
w zapachu ognia i spalonych zbóż.
Pluszczą pontony, tryska ptak zbudzony,
Roz-kwi-ta-ły pęki białych róż.*

Nie śpiewajcie, chłopcy, pieśni tej—
porucznik mówi—bo zanadto smutna
i tak już w wodzie mokniemy po pas.
Nie bójcie się, tam w górze nie szrapnele—
po prostu leci ogień sennych gwiazd.

Mój mały—szepczą dziecku w wiosce siwej
od mgły armatniej—mały, bajkę chcesz?
Więc była... rzeka nazwana Stochodem.
W rzece mieszkała taka ryba, leszcz.

A leszcz był płaski jak miesiąc wieczorem,
i pływał sobie, wodne kwiaty jadł,
aż przyszedł ktoś nad wodę i zakrzyczał:
wróć, u-ca-łuj jak za dawnych lat.**

Zdziwił się leszcz, kto go wołać może.
Ale dość bajki, śpijże już, mój mały.
Jest inna bajka. Był raz sobie kraj,
a w kraju żyta szerokie szumiały,
szumiały żyta, szumiały i szły
krajem pociągi pełne bochnów chleba,
nad pociągami srebrny grał skowronek...
Dalej nie umiem.

("Kołysanka," *TZ*, 26–27)

* The words of a popular soldiers' song; to indicate this quotation marks are used in the English translation.

** A line from the same song.

By pillars smeared with dripping tar
In the province where everyday you hear gun fire,
With the echo of the sappers' song on human fate
A cradle rocks a child's weeping.

It rocks, it hushes a new hero
In the smell of fire and burned wheat.
Pontoons slash, a startled bird takes wing.
"And white roses then were a-blooming."

Don't sing, boys, that song,
Says the lieutenant—it's too depressing.
We are already soaked up to our waists.
Don't be afraid—there, in the sky,
not shrapnels burst, just sleepy stars are aflame.

My little one—they whisper to the child
In a village grey with cannon smoke—
Do you want a tale? There was a river,
In the river a fish lived, a bream.

The bream was flat as an evening moon,
Was swimming and eating water flowers.
Then suddenly someone at the river bank
Began to sing: "Come back, kiss me as in the days of old."

That bream did not know who could call him.
But enough of that tale, sleep my little one.
There is another tale. There was once a land
Where fields of wheat rustled peacefully
And trains moved slowly filled with loaves of bread.
Above the trains a silver skylark trilled.
I don't remember what was next.

("Lullaby," tr. E.M.)

A camera's eye presentation of war gives way in the last stanza to an interesting shift in time perspective of the lyrical subject: although the past tense is used, his voice, in fact, reaches us from the future; the poet darts ahead in his thoughts; he speaks suddenly of fields of wheat which already belong to the past, which is something unreal, like a fairy-tale about a fish (in this case, a bream). Is this a vision of the annihilation of Poland which was to take place a few years later? This is possible, but the poet does not concretize his vision, and thus the verse ends with a terse, laconic sentence: "Dalej nie umiem" ("I don't remember what was next").[5] Three years later, in the poem "Powolna rzeka" ("Slow River") of 1936, a vision of crematoria flashes by:

> —"Ach, ciemna tłuszcza na zielonej runi,
> a krematorja niby białe skały
> i dym wychodzi z gniazd nieżywych os.
> Bełkot mandolin ślad wielkości tłumi,
> na gruzach jadła, nad mech spopielały
> nowego żniwa wschód, kurzawa kos."
>
> ("Powolna rzeka," *TZ*, 36)

> —"Ah, dark rabble at their vernal feasts
> and crematoria rising like white cliffs
> and smoke seeping from the dead wasps' nests.
> In a stammer of mandolins, a dust-cloud of scythes,
> on heaps of food and mosses stomped ash-gray,
> the new sun rises on another day."
>
> ("Slow River," *CP*, 19)

Here is another quotation from the poem "W mojej ojczyźnie" ("In My Native Land"):

> W mojej ojczyźnie, do której nie wrócę,
> Jest takie leśne jezioro ogromne,
> Chmury szerokie, rozdarte, cudowne
> Pamiętam, kiedy wzrok za siebie rzucę.
>
> ("W mojej ojczyźnie," *UP*, 41)

> In my native land where I won't return
> There is a vast forest lake.
> I remember, any time I look back,
> Wide spread clouds, torn, marvelous.
>
> ("In My Native Land," tr. E.M.)

We may conjecture that each of these poems reveals a different aspect of the catastrophic vision: the first concerns the fate of the country; the second speaks of some kind of general extermination; the third expresses a presentiment of personal adversity, of banishment, of emigration from his native land. Such an interpretation is tempting, but it carries within it the danger of oversimplification. Miłosz's catastrophism does not lend itself to identification solely with the prophecy of the imminent Second World War or foretelling of the Polish national tragedy during the years 1939–1945; it cannot be related to any specific historical situation or political event. His catastrophism contains a more profound moral; I would say it is universal or even metaphysical. It is a consequence of the pessimistic perception of the world which dominated Miłosz's views at that time. Miłosz himself aids in qualifying the essence of catastrophism in his book *Ziemia Ulro (The Land of Ulro)* of 1977. Catastrophism, according to the poet, "was above all engaged with the great crisis of civilization. Only later was it acknowledged, somewhat superficially, as a Cassandra-like prophecy of the events of 1939–45, even though the Second World War was but a corollary of a far more protracted crisis."[6] To this remark he adds still another: "Leftist or not, 'catastrophism' was chary of the near future and foresaw decades, if not centuries, of tragedy."[7] Let us add that catastrophism also expressed a crisis in moral norms questioned by contemporary civilization; hence, probably, its pessimism. In *The Land of Ulro*, Miłosz comments that we are living in "a period of collapse of civilization," and that it is not easy to live in such a period. The author of "Kołysanka" makes it clear, however, that his catastrophism, like the catastrophism of another poet Józef Czechowicz, embodied a ray of hope; that it was not a "hopeless vision"; it contained the belief that after a period of "upheavals, cataclysms, changes of planetary dimensions which would continue for an undefined period of time," man would reach "the other shore," that is, would reach some other world. I must admit that I do not perceive this vision of an "other shore" in Miłosz's early poetry. In my opinion, it appears in the poems written during the occupation and published just after the war in 1945 in a volume entitled *Ocalenie* (Rescue). It is difficult to answer with certitude whether this means that the poet recognized the Second World War as a manifestation of the apocalypse, after which a rebirth of the world would take place, or whether the hope flowed from immanent religious or philosophical conviction. The striving towards the "other shore" has remained a fundamental part of his works since that time. And when the poet assures us that he has indeed been a "catastrophist" all his life, it means that his poetry does not express pessimism as much as a dilemma: it oscillates between despair and hope. The latter appears in various forms, whether as an enchantment with the beauty of the world, as in, for example, "Piosenka pasterska" ("Shepherds' Song") or whether as a form of hymn, an invocation in his highly elevated and solemn poem "W Warszawie" ("In Warsaw"), or whether as a reflection upon the complexity of human existence, in "Ucieczka" ("Escape"). I cite here the whole poem "W Warszawie":

Co czynisz na gruzach katedry
Świętego Jana, poeto,
W ten ciepły, wiosenny dzień?

Co myślisz tutaj, gdzie wiatr
Od Wisły wiejąc rozwiewa
Czerwony pył rumowiska?

Przysięgałeś, że nigdy nie będziesz
Płaczką żałobną.
Przysięgałeś, że nigdy nie dotkniesz
Ran wielkich swego narodu,
Abyb nie zmienić ich w świętość,
Przeklętą świętość, co ściga
Przez dalsze wieki potomnych.

Ale ten płacz Antygony,
Co szuka swojego brata,
To jest zaiste nad miarę
Wytrzymałości. A serce
To kamień, w którym jak owad
Zamknięta jest ciemna miłość
Najnieszczęśliwszej ziemi.

Nie chciałem kochać tak,
Nie było to moim zamiarem.
Nie chciałem litować się tak,
Nie było to moim zamiarem.
Moje pióro jest lżejsze
Niż pióro kolibra. To brzemię
Nie jest na moje siły.
Jakże mam mieszkać w tym kraju,
Gdzie noga potrąca o kości

Niepogrzebane najbliższych?
Słyszę głosy, widzę uśmiechy. Nie mogę
Nic napisać, bo pięcioro rąk
Chwyta mi moje pióro
I każe pisać ich dzieje,
Dzieje ich życia i śmierci.
Czyż na to jestem stworzony,
By zostać płaczką żałobną?
Ja chcę opiewać festyny,
Radosne gaje, do których
Wprowadzał mnie Szekspir. Zostawcie
Poetom chwilę radości,
Bo zginie wasz świat.

Szaleństwo tak żyć baz uśmiechu
I dwa powtarzać wyrazy
Zwrócone do was, umarli,
Do was, których udziałem
Miało być wesele
Czynów myśli i ciała, pieśni, uczt.
Dwa ocalone wyrazy:
Prawda i sprawiedliwość.

("W Warszawie," *O*)

What are you doing here, poet, on the ruins
Of St. John's Cathedral this sunny
Day in spring?

What are you thinking here, where the wind
Blowing from the Vistula scatters
The red dust of the rubble?

You swore never to be
a ritual mourner.
You swore never to touch
The deep wounds of your nation
So you would not make them holy
With the accursed holiness that pursues
Descendants for many centuries.

But the lament of Antigone
Searching for her brother

Is indeed beyond the power
Of endurance. And the heart
Is a stone in which is enclosed,
Like an insect, the dark love
Of a most unhappy land.

I did not want to love so,
That was not my design.
I did not want to pity so,
That was not my design.
My pen is lighter
Than a hummingbird's feather. This burden
Is too much for it to bear.
How can I live in this country
Where the foot knocks against
The unburied bones of kin?
I hear voices, see smiles. I cannot
write anything; five hands
Seize my pen
And order me to write
The story of their lives and death.
Was I born to become
A ritual mourner?
I want to sing of festivities,
The greenwood into which Shakespeare
Often took me. Leave
To poets a moment of happiness,
Otherwise your world will perish.

It's madness to live without joy
And to repeat to the dead
Whose part was to be gladness
Of action in thought and in the flesh, singing, feasts,
Only the two salvaged words:
Truth and justice.

Warsaw, 1945
("In Warsaw," *CP*, 79)

The end of the poem signals a realm of issues which, with the passing of time and approaching sociopolitical changes, draw the attention of the poet and become one of the principal motifs of his works: here, his moralizing tone is gathering strength through taking an explicitly dramatic stand which points to the cause of the ongoing struggle and at the same time contains its repudiation. The last stanza of the poem "W malignie" ("In Delirium"), written in 1940, ends thus:

> Pokój na wieki ludziom dobrej woli.
> Wszystkim, co prawdę ziemi poznać chcą.
> Aż, jako ziarno bywa od kąkolu,
> Od dobra będzie oddzielone zło.
>
> ("W malignie," *O*)

> Peace be for ever to men of good will,
> to all who want to learn the truth of the earth,
> till, as a grain is separated from cockles
> good will be separated from evil.
>
> ("In Delirium," tr. E.M.)

Miłosz's conception of the world does not allow for evasions or for the courting of compromise; the poet belongs to those who want to come to know the truth of the earth, because it is a vital, inexhaustible fountainhead of creation; it is the substance of creation. We thus read in the poem "Toast" ("A Toast") the following words:

> A poezja jest prawda. I kto ją obedrze
> Z prawdy, niech jej kupuje trumnę kutą w srebrze.
>
> ("Toast," *SD*)

> Poetry is truth. If you strip it of truth
> you buy for it a silver-wrought coffin.
>
> ("A Toast," tr. E.M.)

What, then, is truth? It is not, in any case, fidelity to the external details of reality, or descriptions of nature which call to mind the realistic depictions of a painter. There is no doubt: the particular, the sensual perception of the world has an important function in Miłosz's poetry, but truth above all means fidelity to one's own experience, convictions and values; it is an incessant striving towards a definition of one's own "I." At the foundation of truth lies a moral assessment of experience. The moral sensibility of the poet often is paired with the dispassionateness of observation.

These general assumptions find their historical concretization. Irena Sławińska, for example, writes that poems such as "Portret z połowy XX wieku" ("Mid-Twentieth-Century Portrait") as well as "Dziecię Europy" ("Child of Europe"), written just after the war, exercised tremendous influence on the older, as well as the younger generation of Poles: they learned the poems by heart, copied them by hand and distributed them among the multitudes of lovers of poetry.[8] Why did they evoke such popularity? Generally speaking, we may acknowledge that they warned of the approaching Stalinist era of duplicity, mendacity and terror. These poems expressed not only the visionary character of Miłosz's poetry, his astonishing perspicacity, his ability to reconcile universal assumptions with historical perspective, but also an intensified tone or sarcasm, irony and bitter accusation. "Portret z połowy XX wieku" presents an image of a person living in a world of double values, of a cynical, double-faced person who "Rękę oparł na pismach Marksa, ale w domu czyta Ewangelię" ["Keeping one hand on Marx's writings, he reads the Bible in private" (*SP,* 58)]. In "Dziecię Europy," the feeling of guilt towards those killed or murdered during the war stems from the fact that those who survived saved themselves at the expense of those who were lost; they escaped death thanks to the shrewdness, the cleverness of a civilization which takes away frankness and honesty and teaches hypocrisy:

> Do wyboru mając śmierć własną i śmierć przyjaciela
> Wybieraliśmy jego śmierć, myśląc zimno: byle się spełniło.
> ("Dziecię Europy," *SD*)

> Having the choice of our own death and that of a friend,
> We chose his, coldly thinking: let it be done quickly.
> ("Child of Europe," *SP,* 59)

Here Miłosz stands forward as a critic of contemporary civilization; he warns that external material well-being does not go hand-in-hand with moral decency. The intensity of this indictment brings to mind another writer, Tadeusz Borowski, who at about the same time wrote with embittered, biting, brutal frankness characteristic of his wartime narratives, although the motivation for such a posture was different in the two cases. The centuries of human evolution towards contemporary civilization which led man to today's refined ways of thought did not teach honesty, but rather deprived man of inner simplicity and sensitivity of warmth, and formed in him a soulless rationalism or cynicism. The eight stanzas of this poem are actually a systematic portrayal of different forms of contemporary mendacity; those who went through the Gehenna of Stalinist casuistry can interpret them today as a reminder of a nightmare.

These verses constitute a link between Miłosz's earlier works and those of the early fifties; they lead to his ultimate break with the communist regime. For those who, in their servility towards the regime, showed him their lack of confidence, these works could without doubt become a pretext for accusing him of a desire to emigrate; emigration ultimately took place in 1951. What were the motives behind this step, which in its time caused political polemics and brought down on Miłosz's head so many thunderbolts and so much censure from a certain section of Poles abroad? He was accused of having decided not to return to Poland for personal reasons, for egoistic writer's motives, for wanting to retain the untouchability of his "aesthetic I." He was slandered with exaggerated aestheticism, as in the opinion of his adversaries his declaration explaining his motives for remaining in the West did not contain expressions of disapproval of the political system in Poland. They even accused him of being double-faced, because they simplified complex problems into the simple argument that when the nation is suffering, a poet should not care only for the preservation of his independence as a writer; he should actively engage himself in the fight against the hated and forcefully imposed dictatorship. Through the perspective of years and in the entire context of Miłosz's known works, how does his choice to emigrate now look? Two articles throw considerable light on this decision: the now-famous "Nie" ("No") and "Poezja i dialektyka" ("Poetry and Dialectics"), printed in consecutive issues of the Paris monthly *Kultura* in May and June, 1951. In fact, Miłosz admits that over a certain period of time he was in agreement with the social changes which took place in postwar Poland, but from the moment "when it was decided to christen me and writers similar to me . . . I said: "No!"[9] What does the word "christen" mean here? Of course it means the imposition of the Soviet doctrine of "socialist realism" as the obligatory norm of artistic creation. From the moment of such a "christening," a writer was considered to be a "socialist realist." This was unacceptable to Miłosz, since the introduction of such a unifying and arbitrary method deprived writers of the right to think, of the right to their own interpretation of the facts and processes of reality. In this connection the poet wrote the following:

> What is meant here is not the right to practise "art for art's sake." We live in times when the [gratification of the] writer's egotism is the worst

> use which can be made of freedom. What is meant here is the right to revolt and to judge laws, customs and institutions. Socialist realism defines in detail how a writer ought to observe, how to select from among his observations, and to which conclusions he should come.[10]

Without doubt, therefore, Miłosz's choice to emigrate was above all an act of moral resistance. All other consequences may be seen as stemming from this decision. The attack by Polish emigrant circles was rather a demonstration of ill will, a misunderstanding, or better said, a lack of understanding of Miłosz's attitude; maybe it was a little of each. A writer was attacked who after the War never besmirched himself by writing one line which could be taken advantage of by the Polish communist regime for the extemporaneous objectives of tactical or political games. It happened thus because he defended the pride of the writer's vocation, that, which in English, is expressed by the untranslatable yet by all means appropriate word "integrity." Miłosz's attitude resulted from a nonconformist understanding of the role of literature; by no means did it result from the substitution of one political doctrine for another ideology, as his critics seemed to demand; for the writer is not a politician but the conscience of his nation, or the collective consciousness of the readership. Here again it is fitting to quote his characteristic remark:

> A writer's ambition should be to touch the simple, honest people who may never have read Proust or Joyce, but who are absorbed by far from insignificant problems.[11]

The battle for "Art" with a capital "A" involves the most intimate inner instincts of the artist; it touches the most fundamental matters resulting from his vision of the world; ". . . the game does not concern undefined 'cultural values'," claimed Miłosz in his article "Poezja i dialektyka":

> On the contrary, the most fundamental human beliefs are engaged here: on the settling of some seemingly completely abstract struggles depends the future of a certain type of civilization and thus the fate of the worker and the peasant as well as the artist.[12]

In his famous article "Nie," Miłosz states that a condition for authenticity of a work of art is not only excellence of artistic craft, but above all its *moral content.* When we examine Miłosz's concept of art more carefully, we see that it is built upon three inseparable elements: 1) truth: the artist should observe reality in such a way that "*nothing* [Miłosz's emphasis] should be lost"; 2) vision: a work has a visionary character; it is "a visionary, specific cognition of reality"; that is, "it moves ahead of the collective consciousness and... discovers new truths"; and 3) integrity: the third component of this conception is the rectitude or integrity of the moral posture of an artist which rejects unconditionally all forms of opportunism, of an artist who does not agree to the betrayal of his creative individuality, neither for material wealth nor on behalf of the most sagacious philosophy or ideology. This, of course, remains in a neat harmony with the principle number one.

From this apolitical conception of art grows one of the most superb political books known to Polish literature, namely *Zniewolony umysł,* published in 1953. The symbols "Alpha," "Beta," "Gamma," and "Delta" are not difficult to decipher. Behind them are hidden Jerzy Andrzejewski, Jerzy Putrament, Tadeusz Borowski and Konstanty Ildefons Gałczyński. Miłosz creates superb literary portraits of these writers and shows the mechanism drawing them into the service of the totalitarian machine of the state, whose subjugation of artists was put forward as one of its paramount and crucial tasks. In spite of a liking for, or even a cordial relationship with some of the above writers, Miłosz did not waver in exposing their "games," their two-edged, not to say two-faced attitude towards the communist rulers. He did so with all the sincerity, however painful, yet indispensible for the revelation of the tragedies not only of Polish intellectuals, but of East European intellectuals in general. Only frankness could bring to the light of day the full dimensions of these tragedies which in more than one case ended in death by suicide.

In one of the first chapters of *Zniewolony umysł,* the author introduces the concept of "ketman." Ketman is a word from Arabic which roughly translates as "hypocrisy" or "conformism."[13] Ketman is the art of deception which consists of passing over things in silence, of hiding one's true feelings towards the ruler while at the same time maintaining a feeling of superiority over him. In the system created by the Soviets, Miłosz differentiates between different types of ketman: national, revolutionary-puritanical, aesthetic, professional, sceptical, metaphysical and ethical. The reader becomes aware that indeed all spheres of life in this artificial, bookish system are redolent with hypocrisy and deception and that the system itself is dependent upon force. It is not only the ruler who is deceived; there is insincerity in communal life, in social relationships, which becomes everyday practice and a principle of survival. Sincerity and truth cannot go hand-in-hand with fear. It is significant that in his description of the problems of the "new faith," or communism, Miłosz restricts himself to areas which he knows well; that is, to literature and art. By analogy, however, and also through the many details spread throughout the work concerning the afflictions or the absurdities of everyday life in the "peoples' republics," a comprehensive picture emerges from this book of a system based on the argument of force and the violation of human dignity. Miłosz was the first writer to make such an extensive, well-ordered analysis of a system imposed by the Soviets on the countries of Eastern and Central Europe and to reveal the depths of its degeneration. In its essence, *Zniewolony umysł* was not to be a political work; rather it was supposed to be a confession, but as it was published at the height of Stalinism and the cold war, it had to become political. It is worth mentioning another paradox connected with the publishing of *Zniewolony umysł:* this book, not being either in the opinion of the author himself, nor in the opinion of the critics, the most important work of his life, brought him renown and for some time obscured the greatness of his poetry. This is not an isolated case in the history of modern literature. One is reminded here of Boris Pasternak, the great Russian poet who became famous for his novel *Doctor Zhivago.*

Whereas *Zniewolony umysł* gave a description of the most general laws of the system of government which was born with the "new faith" and thus could be applied to the situation in all "peoples' democracies," the novel *Zdobycie władzy (The Seizure of Power)* from 1953 brought us to the heartland of Poland. I know of no other work which so comprehensively and bluntly reflects the period during which the communists took power in Poland, so tragic in its consequences. The tragedy of the Warsaw Uprising is shown here, as is the drama of the Polish intelligentsia, the cynicism of the new rulers, the Jewish question and above all the crushing hopelessness, the utter desperation and the dismal atmosphere of the times. All those who lived in Poland during those times will find in *Zdobycie władzy* a part of their own drama, a painful experience stemming from a feeling of powerlessness and of falling into a deep abyss. Jerzy Andrzejewski's *Popiół i diament (Ashes and Diamonds)* dealt with the same period of time, but it gave a false picture of the year 1945–46. It is strange that no one before Miłosz has stated this clearly.[14] When one reads this book, one gets the impression that it was meant as a novel of propaganda for youth under the age of seventeen. In the article "Poezja i dialektyka," Miłosz wrote the following:

> In his novel *Ashes and Diamonds*, my friend Jerzy Andrzejewski allowed himself to depart from the truth about the year 1945, which we spent together in Cracow, as he was staying at the Home of the Writers' Union and had no direct contact with the truly horrifying suffering of this nation in its particulars. In replacing reality with schemata: 1) the depravity of the intelligentsia; 2) youth, or the lost ethic of faithfulness; 3) communists, or the victorious ethic of the social objective, he did not pay the debt which he owed the collective tragedy.[15]

This outstanding debt was paid by Miłosz's novel *Zdobycie władzy* which can be seen as a form of polemics with *Popiół i diament*.[16]

Miłosz's works have a surprising continuity and a consistency rarely found among writers. It is therefore a highly risky undertaking to look for some kind of caesura, for a border separating one period from another in his case. After all, even the aforementioned works, which are the most political of Miłosz's writing, incorporate a historical perspective, a concrete description of occurrences and a universal perception, which in my opinion constitutes the main characteristic of the entire literary output of the author of *Traktat poetycki*. Despite the above statement, it is difficult to resist the temptation to insert certain delimitations. Even the poet himself seems to notice such a caesura, when in the preface *Zniewolony umysł* he admits that the war has changed him considerably. Miłosz writes:

> During the occupation I became more conscious of the social meaning of literature and the Nazi atrocities had a strong influence on the substance of my works; at the same time, my poetry became more understandable, as normally happens when a poet wants to communicate something important to his readers.[17]

It appears that a certain period in Miłosz's creativity comes to an end at the close of the half-century and that a new period begins. The difficulty lies in trying to define the difference. In his article "Społeczne role poety" ("The Social Roles of the Poet"), the Polish critic Janusz Maciejewski distinguishes between two contemporary models of poetry: a) the poet as a judge of reality; and b) the poet as an investigator of reality. He applies this theory to Miłosz's works.[18] Maciejewski believes that in the first period of

Miłosz's creativity there is an overtone of "the poet as a judge of reality" and in the second period, of "the poet as an investigator of reality." The criteria proposed for the establishment of the caesura awaken reservations for various reasons. A "judge" and an "investigator" are present both in the early and in the later period of Miłosz's creativity. The difference consists of a varying accentuation in the two periods. The "poet as investigator of reality" also raises doubts, especially as to the meaning of the last word in the phrase. The question comes to mind: What reality is meant, present or past? Material or metaphysical? The questions keep coming. The word "reality" has been abused so often that it has become hackneyed and must arouse justifiable reservations, especially in works like Miłosz's. The word "reality," as interpreted by J. Maciejewski, does not encompass the visionary character of the poetry of the author of "Traktat moralny" ("A Moral Treatise"); he is a poet who frequently takes us beyond the realm of earthly matters and places us in the presence of ultimate questions. I personally would propose a different criterion for division. It seems to me that somewhere in the mid-fifties, Miłosz's poetic creativity leads in two directions: on the artistic level it achieves an ever greater simplicity; that is, it uses ever more simple means of artistic expression and therefore arrives at a hitherto unknown laconicism and conciseness, whereas in content it takes the direction of further philosophizing: it takes us into the sphere of metaphysics; it is ever more fascinated by the mysteries of human existence and, let us not hesitate to use the phrase, a knowledge of God. Nobody noticed this as aptly as Stefan Cardinal Wyszyński, the late Primate of Poland, in his message to the participants in the ceremony during which the Catholic University of Lublin conferred an honorary doctorate on Czesław Miłosz:

> In the effort of lonely navigation through history the man named Czesław Miłosz is supported by a vision of God Incarnate, which exists in each deliverance of man from bondage.[19]

It is therefore necessary to state clearly that Miłosz's reality is a multifarious reality, or rather a multidimensional one; and therefore his approbation of Einstein's theories should not surprise us. With his outlook, Miłosz encompasses the most opposed, sometimes even contradictory, phenomena of the world; he combines in his works widely separated elements which, it would appear, cannot be reconciled. Thus, regardless of the affects of the writer's individuality and harmony of vision, this poetry is without question difficult to interpret. Both the spiritual and material phenomena of our time are encountered; there are reflections of past and present, of culture and civilization, of the individual and the collectivity, of universality and temporality. Polyphony as a creative principle, so apparent in "Głosy biednych ludzi" ("Voices of Miserable People"), for example, remains one of the foremost characteristics of Miłosz's poetry.

Miłosz believes in the world's metaphysical order. In this respect he is heir to the European romantic tradition and its Polish counterpart. This metaphysical character of Miłosz's poetry often reveals itself in the form of a dichotomy between the physical world and the spiritual world. Behind the sensuality, the physical tangibility of his many poems, is often hidden some other unknown and inscrutable order. In the poem "Wiara" ("Faith") from the cycle "Świat (poema naiwne)" ("The World (A Naive Poem)") we read the same avowal:

> Wiara jest wtedy, kiedy ktoś zobaczy
> Listek na wodzie albo kroplę rosy
> I wie, że one są— bo są konieczne.
> . . . .
> . . . .
> . . . .
>
> Wiara jest także, jeżeli ktoś zrani
> Nogę kamieniem i wie, że kamienie
> Są po to, żeby nogi nam raniły.
>
> ("Wiara," *O*)

> The word *Faith* means when someone sees
> A dewdrop or a floating leaf, and knows
> That they are, because they have to be.
> . . . .
> . . . .
> . . . .
>
> It means that when someone's foot is hurt
> By a sharp rock, he also knows that rocks
> Are here so that they can hurt our feet.
>
> ("Faith," *SN*, 143–44)

The same motif will be heard again in the novel *Dolina Issy (The Issa Valley)*. One of the characters says:

> "Take an oak. Any oak in the forest. You look at it standing there, and what do you think? That it's where it ought to be, that place and no other. Right?"
>
> "Right."
>
> "But supposing the acorn was dug up and eaten by a wild pig. Would you still look down at the ground and say an oak tree belonged there?" . . .
>
> "No. Why not? Because once the thing is, it's like it had to be that way always, always and forever. Same as with a man."[20]

In one of the relatively new poems, the order of physical existence is accepted as a gift which combines with a feeling of inner cheerfulness and happiness:

> Dzień taki szczęśliwy.
> Mgła opadła wcześnie, pracowałem w ogrodzie.
> Kolibry przystawały nad kwiatem kaprifolium.
> Nie było na ziemi rzeczy, którą chciałbym mieć.
> Nie znałem nikogo, komu warto byłoby zazdrościć.
> Co przydarzyło się złego, zapomniałem.
> Nie wstydziłem się myśleć, że byłem kim jestem.
> Nie czułem w ciele żadnego bólu.
> Prostując się, widziałem niebieskie morze i żagle.
>
> ("Dar," *GWS*)

> A day so happy.
> Fog lifted early, I worked in the garden.
> Hummingbirds were stopping over honeysuckle flowers.
> There was no thing on earth I wanted to possess.
> I knew no one worth my envying him.
> Whatever evil I had suffered, I forgot.
> To think that once I was the same man did not embarrass me.
> In my body I felt no pain.
> When straightening up, I saw the blue sea and sails.
>
> ("Gift," *SP*, 117)

It would be a mistake to think that by accepting the world in this way the poet solves the dilemmas of existence. Evil and good remain inseparable parts of our existence; evil appears in the form of wrong and pain. Existence is suffering, but this does not mean that one must accept the suffering. Miłosz's creativity from the mature years contains a large number of allusions directed against injustice, mendacity, hypocrisy, violence, and the abasement of human dignity. Sometimes these allusions take a general, philosophical form; sometimes they are concrete, referring to a specific situation. In the poem "Rady" ("Counsels"), for example, we have the following stanza:

> Człowiekowi potrafiono dać do zrozumienia,
> że jeżeli żyje, to tylko z łaski potężnych.
> Niech więc zajmie się piciem kawy i łowieniem motyli.
> Kto kocha Rzecz Pospolitą, będzie miał dłon uciętą.
>
> ("Rady," *MBI*)

> Man has been given to understand
> that he lives only by the grace of those in power.
> Let him therefore busy himself sipping coffee, catching butterflies.
> Who cares for the Republic will have his right hand cut off.
>
> ("Counsels," *SP*, 109)

In order to understand the bitter irony of these words and the anger they contain, it is necessary to remember that they are an allusion to the infamous memory of Józef Cyrankiewicz, for many years premier of the Polish People's Republic. After the incidents in Poznań, in 1956, he threatened, in one of his speeches, that those who raise their hand against the "people's republic" would have the hand cut off.

Miłosz's poetic world is far removed from the idyllic. It is filled with sharp contradictions and questions difficult to answer. I have already mentioned that the lyrical hero of this poetry is torn between despair and hope. Speaking of this despair, the poet in *The Land of Ulro* makes the following confession:

> Had I not known tragedy, both private and public, and if most of my life had I not been a struggle at the scream's edge, I too would have found nothing there.[21]

Yet *Ziema Ulro* is itself a symbol of suffering and loneliness in which the poet has long since lived, as he himself admits. Whence, then, may one draw hope? Here we touch the most difficult point in Miłosz's philosophy of life; I would not pretend to give a satisfactory answer to the question. It seems, however, that the answer must be sought in Miłosz's growing interest in metaphysical and religious problems. It also lies in his belief about the return of the past, so clearly stated in the Charles Eliot Norton lectures published under the title *The Witness of Poetry:*

> Earlier I spoke of the lessons of biology and of reductionist *Weltanschauung* professed universally today. I expressed the hope that it will be superseded by another vision better adapted to the complexity of the world and of individuals. It seems to me that this will be connected, in one or another way, with a new dimension entered on by elemental humanity—and here I expect some surprise from my audience—the dimension of the past of our human race.[22]

This visionary interest is also apparent in the collection of poems *Miasto bez imienia* (City Without a Name) from 1969 and in *Gdzie wschodzi słońce i kędy zapada* (From Where the Sun Rises to Where It Sets) from 1974. Generally speaking, the poet draws strength, hope and cheerfulness of spirit from the moral norms laid down by Christianity; for Miłosz, however, these norms are not a stiff structure of behaviour hardened in dogma. It is not an acceptance without reservation, a taking of the easy road. The difficulty stems from the fact that we live in times in which God does not reveal outward signs of His presence:

> Nie myślałem, że żyć będę w tak osobliwej chwili.
> Kiedy Bóg skalnych wyżyn i gromów,
> Pan Zastępów, kyrios Sabaoth,
> Najdotkliwiej upokorzy ludzi,
> Pozwoliwszy im działać jak tylko zapragną,
> Im zostawiając wnioski i nie mówiąc nic.
>
> ("Oeconomia Divina," *GWS*)

> I did not expect to live in such an unusual moment,
> When the God of thunders and of rocky heights,
> The Lord of hosts, Kyrios Sabaoth,
> Would humble people to the quick,

allowing them to act whatever way they wished,
leaving to them conclusions, saying nothing.
("Oeconomia Divina," *SP*, 106)

In "Veni Creator" he adds:

Prosiłem nieraz, wiesz sam, żeby figura w kościele
podniosła dla mnie rękę, raz jeden jedyny.
Ale rozumiem że znaki mogą być tylko ludzkie.
Zbudź więc jednego człowieka, gdziekolwiek na ziemi
(nie mnie, bo jednak znam co przyzwoitość)
i pozwól abym patrząc na niego podziwiać mógł Ciebie.
("Veni Creator," *MBI*)

Many a time I asked, you know it well, that the statue in church
lift its hand, only once, just once, for me.
But I understand that signs must be human,
therefore call one man, anywhere on earth,
not me—after all I have some decency—
and allow me, when I look at him, to marvel at you.
("Veni Creator," *SN*, 183)

This is a situation which might be called troublesome, but it does not evoke in Miłosz's lyrical hero a doubt in the existence of God. Thus with justification the late Primate Stefan Cardinal Wyszyński speaks of "the warm and human presence of God" in the poetry of the author of *Ziemia Ulro*. Two books seem to be important for an understanding of Miłosz' works: *Rodzinna Europa* (1958) (*Native Realm*) and *Ziemia Ulro* (1977). To the extent that the former clarifies the sources which formed his poetic individuality, the latter throws light on his philosophical *credo* as it has developed during the past twenty years of his writing.

When Miłosz decided to emigrate, he judged that he was committing suicide as a writer. The history of his creativity in the past thirty years is a complete denial of such misgivings. In this period six volumes of poetry, two novels and ten volumes of essays on literary, philosophical and aesthetic questions were published. The unusually significant role of the Paris periodical *Kultura*, a Polish literary monthly, cannot be passed over in silence; it opened its columns to Miłosz and, thanks to the untiring energy of its editor, J. Giedroyc, made possible the publishing of his works in book form. In addition, two works were written in English: *The History of Polish Literature* (1969) and *The Emperor of the Earth: Modes of Eccentric Vision* (1978).

It is an impressive literary output, testifying to the writer's unusual diligence. His essays touch upon a variety of important issues of our time. They contain a reevaluation of the cultural heritage, polemics with contemporary literary and philosophical trends still in vogue (Marxism and Existentialism), but above all they combine a freshness of outlook with an erudition rarely encountered today. The form of construction of these essays should in future become the subject of a special study of the aesthetics of literary sketches.[23] Miłosz displays a piety and an attachment to tradition which is rare today. It is apparent not only in his literary-critical works on Polish, English, French and American literature but manifests itself with particular artistry in his poetry.

In connection with this, another term which is associated with Miłosz's works, the Classicism of poetry, requires explanation. The term is also used when referring to such twentieth-century poets as T.S. Eliot or Osip Mandelstam.[24] It is known in other domains of art, for example, in music. Classicism entails a deep attachment to tradition combined with a disciplined treatment of poetic discourse and concreteness of presentation which at times brings to mind realism. The works of those artists who are regarded as classicists are, so to speak, generated by the realities of our heritage in the art of the past and by the realities of culture in its different spheres and in its various epochs. Consequently, they display unusually strong intensity of metatextual correlations. Miłosz himself wrote the following:

> Many a time . . . I pondered over Classicism, or rather over the reoccurring temptation of Classicism in European culture. In its mature versions it is literature nourished by literature, because the striving to achieve the heights of perfection demands the distillation of what has been handed over by predecessors, because more important in this case is the relation of the apprentice to the master than a writer's relation to the surrounding objects.[25]

One should not be misled by the final remark in the above citation. It is true: the modern classicist strives toward integrating within his own poetic vision traditional values of the past (myths, religious thought, aesthetic conventions, social, political concepts as they occurred in literature or folklore). He is exceptionally concerned with the strictly literary nature of poetry, and hence, a much stronger degree of "literariness" is inherent in his works. Yet, at the same time, he subjects all these poetic components to his own intellectual scrutiny and confronts them with his own epoch, with contemporary questions of human existence. Hence the transcendental, meditative, philosophical, and, at times, pessimistic or apocalyptic tone of this poetry. The art of today's classicists is not always easy to understand and the reader's encounter with it means a continuous intellectual challenge. Whether a writer or a composer, both have their roots in the ample and varied tradition. The syncretic character of this poetry creates, no doubt, difficulty in reception: it requires of readers extensive reading and considerable knowledge of the cultural past. Miłosz's multidimensional Classicism is in this respect no exception, and, I would suggest, constitutes an especially complex case.

The impulse to foster a programme of Classicism (to be sure, Miłosz never clearly formulated such a programme), or rather the impulse to practise literary Classicism in a more conscious way came probably from the works of Anglo-American poets such as T.S. Eliot, W.H. Auden, and K. Shapiro (for example, in the latter's *Essay on Rime*). His classical tendency manifests itself in a striving for precision, for a clarity stemming from the internal cohesion and logic of the text. Other manifestations of the classical tendency are the striving of the poet to maintain a distance between himself and the lyrical subject, that is, a nonidentification of these two notions; the renewed use of long poetic forms which are capable of undertaking great philosophical, religious themes, themes of civilization and of art in general in order that he be able to "speak directly." The realization of these creative principles may be found in many of Miłosz's works, especially in "Traktat moralny" (1947), "Toast" (1949), *Traktat poetycki* (1957) and *The Witness of Poetry* (1983). The latter collection of Miłosz's lectures at Harvard is particularly revealing with regard to his understanding of poetry and its role in modern society. The poet laments the existing abyss between writers and readers, an abyss that occurred for the first time at the turn of the century. He rejects the idea of "pure poetry," aestheticism and extreme pessimism which express sterile impotence and lack of hope. Miłosz definitely declares himself to be on the side of "poetry of *content*." This is precisely the main thrust of modern classicist aesthetics.

A few words must be said about *Traktat poetycki.* In the annals of twentieth-century Polish literature, this is the most ambitious and the most significant poetic work because thematically it encompasses both recent Polish history and recent Polish literature, as well as philosophical considerations and religious motifs. It is a poem of digression *par excellence* in which we perceive the poet's tone of moral commitment, his concern for the fate of the world and his description of Poland's tragedy. In the sense that a Polish theme is undertaken on a wider, generalized scale, this is probably the most "Polish" of Miłosz's works. The tragedy of the country is at once his tragedy:

> Na jakże długo starczy mi nonsensu
> Polski, gdzie pisze się poezję wzruszeń
> Z ograniczoną odpowiedzialnością?
> Chcę nie poezji, ale dykcji nowej.
> Bo tylko ona pozwoli wyrazić
> Tę nową czułość, a w niej ocalenie
> Od prawa, które nie jest naszym prawem,
> Od konieczności, która nie jest nasza,
> Choćbyśmy nasze jej nadali imię.
>
> (*TP*)

> For how long I will acquiesce in the nonsense
> of Poland, where they write poetry of feelings
> With a limited responsibility?
> I do not want poetry, but a new diction.
> For only it enables us to express
> That new openness liberating us
> From a law that is not a law of ours,
> Even if we were willing to give it our name.
>
> ("Poetic Treatise," tr. E.M.)

At the same time, however, these lines are not devoid of irony aimed at the "poetry of feelings with a limited responsibility." This may imply either a literature of antiquated sensibility, or a literature constrained by ideological factors. The poet pleads for a "new diction," speaking against the historical situation imposed on his nation by others. Here, both history and literature are intertwined in a masterly, subtle manner, and the writer is seen as someone at variance with the existing conditions.

Both the understanding of tradition and its utilization have a syncretic character in Miłosz's works. In "List półprywatny o poezji" ("A Semiprivate Letter on Poetry") he wrote the following:

> One should feel sorry that in Poland, whenever somebody wants to speak on so-called "great themes," he falls into the romantic manner, which allegedly shows his fidelity to tradition, but to a tradition from which many centuries have been cut off.[26]

Apparent in his works is a great admiration for A. Mickiewicz, but also an equally deep attachment to his kinsman, the French poet Oscar de Milosz, to the Swedish scholar and philosopher Emanuel Swedenborg, the English poet W. Blake, the Russian Feodor Dostoyevski; to the Manichaeism and its Slavic extension, Bogomilism. This list is indeed imposing, yet it can be supplemented by adding more recent writers, such as for example Lev Shestov or the French writer Simone Weil. At the same time, however, in *The Land of Ulro* Miłosz makes the following admission:

> If I were asked to name the source of my poetry, I would have to answer: my childhood, which was a childhood of carols, Month of Mary devotions, vespers—and of the Protestant Bible, the only one then available.[27]

In other words, his poetry is open to the effects of different strata of culture, having begun from the most elementary and popular which we absorb in the years of childhood and ending with the most complex ethical, aesthetic and philosophical systems. I would not want to be misunderstood here: I do not mean influences, but the creative utilization of the past. Miłosz's Classicism is undogmatic, drawing from the most varied sources of the past. His sensitivity to such diverse strata of tradition should not surprise us. He was born and raised in a multilingual and multicultural environment among Poles, Lithuanians, White Russians, Jews and Russians; thus the poet's firm solidarity with these national groups (with the exception of the Russians as a nation) and his frequent appearances as their spokesman and defender, seeking redress for their violated rights. This is especially apparent in his speech on the occasion of receiving the Nobel Prize.

Let us sum up our reflections and answer a difficult question: what makes this poet so fascinating and great? It seems that Miłosz, as no other poet, has addressed those issues which, for our epoch, are the most fundamental and essential: 1) the crisis of contemporary civilization and its slow disintegration; 2) defense of the individual; a defense of the individuality and dignity of man faced with the dismal spectre of totalitarianism. This defense carries with it a ray of hope; it rejects existentialist nihilism and develops an affection for the values of the Judeo-Christian tradition; it embraces the various aspects of the tradition; that is, religion, philosophy and culture. In my opinion this is the most stimulating and human current in Miłosz's poetry, restoring faith in the sense of our existence. When we come into contact with this current we get the impression that we are drawing from a clear, undefiled well of wisdom, faith, goodness, and love.

Notes

1. See K. Dybciak, "Tak czytano Miłosza," *Przegląd powszechny*, no. 4 (1981), p. 63–72. Quotation translated by E. Możejko.
2. Only recently, J. Błoński addressed the question of "ethical foundations" of Miłosz's poetry in his article "Muzyka późnych lat albo o formie moralnej," *Tygodnik powszechny*, no. 27 (1986).
3. Cz. Miłosz has translated this term (which linguistically stems from the Lithuanian) as "brashwood" or "dry twigs half charred in the fire but still glowing." See his *The History of Polish Literature* (London: Macmillan, 1969), p. 412.
4. A detailed discussion of these trends can be found in B. Carpenter, *The Poetic Avant-Garde in Poland* (Seattle: University of Washington Press, 1983), p. 234
5. For a more detailed analysis of "Kołysanka" see J.J. Lipski, "Kołysanka" in Cz. Miłosz, *Trzy zimy & Głosy o wierszach* (London: Aneks, 1987(reprint)). Included is a section of critical articles on Miłosz's poetry under the title "Głosy o wierszach" (Voices on Poems), R. Gorczyńska and P. Kłoczowski, eds. The article I refer to appears on pp. 104–6.
6. Cz. Miłosz, *The Land of Ulro* (New York: Farrar Strauss Giroux, 1984), p. 271. For the original see Cz. Miłosz, *Ziemia Ulro* (Paris: Instytut Literacki, 1977), p. 208.
7. Miłosz, *The Land of Ulro*, p. 272; and for the original see Miłosz, *Ziemia Ulro*, pp. 208–9.
8. I. Sławińska, "The Image of the Poet and His Estate," *World Literature Today* 52, no. 3 (Summer 1978), p. 396.
9. See Cz. Miłosz, "Nie," *Kultura*, Paris, no. 5 (1951), p. 4 for the original. Translation by E. Możejko.
10. Ibid., p. 7. Translation by E. Możejko.
11. Ibid., p. 5. Translation by E. Możejko.
12. See Cz. Miłosz, "Poezja i dialektyka," *Kultura*, Paris, no. 6 (1951), p. 32 for the original. Translation by E. Możejko.

13. T. Venclova, "Czesław Miłosz: Despair and Grace," *World Literature Today* 52, no. 3 (Summer 1978), p. 394.
14. More than thirty years later, in the article "Popiół? Diament?", S. Mrożek subjected Andrzejewski's novel to severe criticism. See the Paris monthly *Kultura*, nos. 1–2 (1983), pp. 33–41.
15. For the original see Miłosz, "Poezja i dialektyka," p. 38. Translation by E. Możejko.
16. Prof. M. Levine writes of this in her penetrating study "Warning to the West: Miłosz's Political Prose of the Fifties," included in this volume.
17. For the original see Cz. Miłosz, *Zniewolony umysł* (Paris: Instytut Literacki, 1953), p. 14. Translation from the original Polish edition Preface by E. Możejko.
18. J. Maciejewski, "Społeczne role poety," *Literatura*, no. 35 (1981), p. 12.
19. Stefan Kardynał Wyszyński, "Do świadków promocji doktorskiej Laureata Nagrody Nobla Czesława Miłosza," *Kultura*, nos. 7–8 (1981), p. 15. Quotation translated by E. Możejko.
20. Cz. Miłosz, *The Issa Valley*, tr. by Louis Iribarne (New York: Farrar Straus Giroux, 1981), p. 160. For the original see Cz. Miłosz, *Dolina Issy* (Paris: Instytut Literacki, 1979), p. 110.
21. Miłosz, *The Land of Ulro*, p. 212. For the original see Miłosz, *Ziemia Ulro*, p. 166.
22. Cz. Miłosz, *The Witness of Poetry, The Charles Eliot Norton Lectures of* 1981–82 (Cambridge, Mass.: Harvard University Press, 1983), p. 109. It also appears in Polish under the title *Świadectwo poezji. Sześć wykładow o dotkliwościach naszego wieku* (Paris: Instytut Literacki, 1983), 93 p.
23. Quite a few articles about Miłosz as an essayist were published by Polish critics in the early eighties: K. Pieńkosz, "Gdzie wschodzi słońce i kędy zpada," *Literatura* 10, no. 5 [467] (1981), p. 12; A. Kijowski, "Tematy Miłosza," *Twórczość* 37, no. 6 [431] (1981), pp. 33–44; K. Mętrak, "Cztery glosy do Miłosza," *Literatura* 10, no. 14 [476] (1981), pp. 7, 12; J. Pieszczachowicz, "Okolice Ulro," *Literatura* 2, no. 12 [15] (1983), pp. 12–14.
24. E. Możejko, "Two Versions of Classicism: O. Mandelstam and T.S. Eliot," *Russian Language Journal* 40 (1986), pp. 111–21.
25. Cz. Miłosz, "O niewiedzy, wyuczonej i literackiej," *Kultura* 6 (1980), pp. 30–31. Translation by E. Możejko.
26. Cz. Miłosz, "List półprywatny o poezji," in *Kontynenty* (Paris: Instytut Literacki, 1958), p. 70.
27. Miłosz, *The Land of Ulro*, p. 248. For the original see Cz. Miłosz, *Ziemia Ulro*, p. 191.

STANISŁAW BEREŚ

Czesław Miłosz's Apocalypse[1]

It is obvious even at first glance that Miłosz's second volume of poetry quite fundamentally from *Poemat o czasie zastygłym* (Poem on Time Frozen). While the postulates with which the Żagarists made their debut were within the realm of experience of "social" poetry, their second phase of artistic development—which is associated primarily with three works: Zagórski's *Przyjście wroga* (The Coming of the Enemy), A. Rymkiewicz's *Tropiciel* (The Pathfinder) and Miłosz's *Trzy zimy* (Three Winters)—was characterized by a remarkably developed visionariness, dreaminess, unbridled baroque associations, as well as restless and agitated imagery. They combined to form a totally unique projection of the world of the Apocalypse transmitted through the filter of individual imagination. This world is defined not so much by a dark foreboding of the extermination which threatens it, but rather by the unwavering certainty (which in these poems still belongs to the sphere of artistic fiction) that it will have to rediscover its material equivalent on the plane of reality. The catastrophic visions of the Żagarists are woven from imaginative dreams, presentiments, moods, fears and a symbolic system for which it is pointless to seek unambiguous semantic equivalents. This entire imaginary world, constructed from poetical phantasmagoria, is ruled only by the laws of the authors' restless imagination. In the face of uncertainties and with a sense of the absurdity of an existence doomed to destruction, the authors turned away from the "visible" world and escaped into realms subject to their incontrovertible creative dictates and causative aesthetic voluntarism. The tragic situation of the Israeli nation at the time of Antiochus IV Epiphanes forced the authors of the classical apocalypses to turn towards a transsensual world and to develop mysterious images and symbols with fantastic or blatantly fairy tale features, built upon dream images and digressions on the subject of numbers, stellar configurations and angels and devils. Similarly, the uncertain reality of the first half of the 1930s in Poland seemed to throw itself into the field of the poetic prophecies of the young writers from the literary group "Żagary."

Each of the three poets named above took a slightly different road. Zagórski, building his volume from records of dream hallucinations with which he was visited around 1934, constructed a grotesque vision of a world tormented by the Antichrist who intervenes in all spheres of human activity. This leads to a situation in which reality is transformed into an unexampled cultural pandemonium devoid of norms, principles and values, disintegrating from the senseless actions of individuals and deviated collectives. Rymkiewicz, for his part, stunned the world he himself had called into existence through the destructive actions of a demonic Pathfinder, who soars like a comet among galaxies and above the parched, sandy Earth, and paralyzes the rotations of the heavenly spheres, causing dread, death and destruction.

At this point one should ask what type of postulates we will discover in Miłosz's works. In his discussion of the first collection of Miłosz's poems, J. Kwiatkowski was already indicating that *Trzy zimy* is that phase in the development of a poet in which the individual begins to dominate over society, the duty of art becomes greater than the obligations towards humanity and "pure" poetry takes precedence over creation with utilitarian aims. This is a phase in which the poet immerses himself in unbridled symbolist visions which are highly resistant to explicit definition due to the already mentioned incredible table of fantastic images, of apprehensions and visions sometimes barely suggested and sometimes clearly explicated. When these visions do not achieve complete aesthetic crystallization, they then spill over into the next, which is equally foggy and difficult to comprehend. It is a complexly woven and unusual poetic garden.

K. Wyka entitled his essay on Miłosz's *Ocalenie* (Rescue) "Ogrody lunatyczne i ogrody pasterskie" ("Lunatic Gardens and Pastoral Gardens"). The poetry of *Trzy zimy* is precisely that lunatic garden, "a dominion of deaf dreams" filled with a "maelstrom of images tangled like tropical vegetation." At the same time these are images which, because of their intangibility, seem to mock the reader who would impute to them definitive precise meanings. Sometimes we have the impression of being in contact with some sort of rare poetic polyp which, being self-sufficient, nourishes ever newer image segments of itself. They grow out from themselves like successive layers of growths—summoned to life by Miłosz's demiurgic imagination. Such are the gloomy images of this strange and terrifying poetic world as it rises multiplying layer upon layer, so difficult to control and comprehend. A state of incessant tension is maintained between this universe of the imagination and the reality which summons it to life. One might say that *Trzy zimy* in its unrestrained catastrophism—since the reality which the poet constructs is branded with the stigma of extermination—is removed from everything by which it was actually determined. That is only an apparent truth, however, since this convoluted poetics very suggestively reflects the absurdity of the political and social situation in Europe between the two World Wars, axiological chaos, the disorder of historical processes and, finally, the tragic aspect of the fate of a poet who tries to restrain this world and to give it adequate artistic expression. On the other hand, however, this work is an expression of the longing of the artist for the opportunity to throw off the restrictions of reality and to create an integral poetic reality, the rules, "form" and ontological status of which could rest only in the hands of a literary Pantocrator who is freely able, as he professes in "Powolna rzeka" ("Slow River"), to rule over an unreal reality formed just as one squeezes objects from clay.

Dreaminess, surrealism, romantic "*creationism,*" avant-garde equivocation of meanings and ecstatic "world-creation," all these form, as it were, one passageway of this poetic flight into an imaginary land with an apocalyptic lining. Several poems such as: "Kołysanka" (Lullaby), "Wieczorem wiatr" ("Wind in the Evening"), "Siena" ("Sienna"), "Ty silna noc" ("You Powerful Night"), which are more condensed and rooted in reality and which present a characteristic type of restrained lyricism and a subdued system of images and metaphors, seem to mark off another such passageway. This lyricism is of the highest order: spontaneous, yet intellectually sophisticated; poetic, yet devoid of sentimentalism; tender, yet not trivial. Both of these currents, however, flow in one direction—in the direction of a world shifted in relation to the reality which limits and unsettles the poet, in the direction of a world not free from the "earthly" menace, yet escaping its destructive might. That world is, after all, diagnosis and recognition, protest and response, a realm of individual freedom suspended above the totalitarianism of reality. However, it is suspended only by the frail threads which are at the disposal of human imagination, deluding itself with the illusion that it is possible to exist more safely in a fiction than in reality.

This expedition into a Hades of half-awake dreams, into a fantastic vision and a "pure" creation not subjected to the correction of threatening reality, would seem to be an expression of the humanistic belief that even in the most horrifying world there is a possibility of creating an ecological niche, a sort of constructive counterproposal to a world off its hinges. How does Miłosz in *Trzy zimy,* while seeking at least aesthetic freedom in a world threatened by catastrophe and yet developing a startling eschatological vision, seek salvation for man and his imagination? How does he renew the controversy over value; where does he discern a chance for the human individual seeking the light of truth?

It is a truism to mention that Miłosz's poetry takes pleasure in oppositions, of antinomical juxtapositions and dialectical opalescence, nevertheless it is difficult not to recall these facts while bent over the pages of the least unambiguous of Miłosz's works. We are seldom made aware of treading on such uncertain and miry ground. A rare few of the enunciations growing out of this visionary glebe can be easily defended and unambivalently explicated.

> Here all the beliefs and all illusions are tried without distinction and, if incompatible with the pulsing of predatory blood, are thrown aside contemptuously on the rubbish heap of the centuries, added to the accumulated mountain of refuse and rubble. . . . It is an unmediated dispute with the world, dressed in symbolic robes, in code, in signs difficult or impossible to make out completely; this is a two-handed struggle with the tangibility of flexed muscles, centuries old, it is an eternal ever self-renewing Jacobean struggle.[2]

The sense of profound ambivalence which the reasons presented here, have as well as the immanent heterogeneity of figurative declarations, make it difficult to assume that Miłosz actually did confine himself to a creative alienation from experiential reality, and that, usurping the right to move the poetic cosmos as if he were an all-powerful cosmocrator, he had recognized this type of aesthetic freedom as sufficient. Many things would seem to speak in favour of this:

> Tobie panowanie,
> tobie obłoki w złoconych pierścionkach
> grają, na drogach słowa szepcą klony,
> od każdej żywej istoty przebiega
> do twoich dłoni niewidzialna uzda—
> targniesz—i wszystko zakręca w pólkole
>
> ("Powolna rzeka," *TZ*, 35)

> .... To you the rule,
> for you clouds in golden rings
> play a music, maples by the road exalt you.
> The invisible rein on every living thing
> leads to your hand—pull, and they all
> turn a half-circle under the canopy
> called cirrus.
>
> ("Slow River," *CP*, 18)

Truly romantic demiurgism, descended from "The Great Improvisation," underlined by a sense of spiritual authority, seems to describe this model of poetic mission, inherited from nineteenth-century prophetism. Having been lifted up above society, a "revealer" makes manifest the verdicts known only to him of an ominous fate, and outlining the images of a disintegrating world of values, shows the devastation of hitherto forms of existence and humanity being transformed into a herd overcome by biologism and in hedonistic spasms amidst the gardens of its crumbling civilization.

> —"Ach, ciemna tłuszcza na zielonej runi,
> a krematoria niby białe skały
> i dym wychodzi z gniazd nieżywych os.
> Bełkot mandolin ślad wielkości tłumi,
> na gruzach jadła, nad mech spopielały
> nowego żniwa wschód, kurzawa kos."
>
> ("Powolna rzeka," *TZ*, 36)

> —"Ah, dark rabble at their vernal feasts
> and crematoria rising like white cliffs

and smoke seeping from the dead wasps' nests.
In a stammer of mandolins, a dust-cloud of scythes,
on heaps of food and mosses stomped ash-gray,
the new sun rises on another day."

("Slow River," *CP*, 19)

The prophecy is, however, strangely concrete, more reminiscent of a poetic news coverage from some little village only recently occupied by enemy forces, and celebrating in a meadow amidst burnt-out beehives and devastated orchards to the accompaniment of wild music, than of symbolic glossolalia. This fragment seems to be a poetic reference to the events of 1920, to images of the weakness and bestiality of man. Of course, this poem is neither "pure" creative projection nor poeticized journalism. It is difficult even to determine to what extent it approaches these two possible types of presentation. The internal ambivalence of this lyric poetry suggests that Miłosz, by contrasting such divergent types of formulations and by weaving them together within the framework of one dominant line of thought or imagery, is striving to create a value which is "articulated" in terms of aesthetics and a philosophy of life. Let us therefore note: neither "pure" journalistic reporting nor "pure" prophecy, but something totally different. This is neither a "coming down to the earth" of social injustice nor an "angelic" escape into the world, from which perspective people seem like puppets moved by the poet's network of imaginary strings.

Potrzykroć winno się obrócić koło
ludzkich zaślepień, zanim ja bez lęku
spojrzę na władzę, śpiącą w moim ręku,

("Powolna rzeka," *TZ*, 37)

Three times must the wheel of blindness
turn, before I look without fear at the power
sleeping in my own hand,

("Slow River," *CP*, 20)

A romantic poet would not likely have written this. These could be the words of a contemporary writer who is becoming aware of the might of the artistic word and of the power it exerts, but nevertheless already realizes how far it can be utilized in establishing paths towards a nonhuman reality.

Potrzykroć muszą zwyciężyć kłamliwi
zanim się prawda wielka nie ożywi

("Powolna rzeka," *TZ*, 37)

Three times will the liars have conquered
before the great truth appears alive

("Slow River," *CP*, 20)

says Miłosz at the end of the poem. This is, of course, the voice of the visionary from Patmos, exposing the dreary outlines of the future, but at the same time a declaration of a contemporary artist who knows how the word of social "revelations" can and, on the basis of the determinism of events, even must, be used. The poet is entangled in the strategies of a multiplicity of conceptions and philosophies designed to endow man with happiness. But these strategies, in fact, lead to horizons beyond which are hidden the contours of a world, terrifying in the dimness of its perspectives, and the poet begins to doubt the unequivocal meaning of his poetic mission. Articulating his "truths," he suddenly notices that they have not been serving those gods to whom they were being addressed, and that falseness has, to his surprise, become a part of his artistic mission.

a kłamstwa mego najpiękniejsze farby
zakryły prawdę. Wtedy spuszczam oczy
i czuję wicher, co przeze mnie wieje
palący, suchy.

("Obłoki," *TZ*, 40)

And that the most beautiful colors of my lie
Veil the truth. Then I cast down my eyes
And feel the wind blow through me,
Burning and dry.

("White Clouds," tr. E.M.)

The poet's autothematic reflections, expressed casually on the pages of *Trzy zimy*, are permeated with a spirit of negation towards hitherto existing forms of communication with the reader. The account is, however, deeply private, carried out in a spirit of humility and trust in the expiation which is attainable, on condition that the poet becomes aware of the new goals assigned to by time. "Dziś ja, uczeń poznałem nicość form powabnych," ("Do kzięḑza Ch.," *TZ*, 50) ["Today, I, the pupil, learned the nothingness of alluring forms," ("To Father Ch.," tr. A.R.)] Miłosz admits to the prefect, contritely confessing his absolutization of biological existence and his affirmation of an art which has too often become its spokesman.

> . . . A sztuka zaklęcia,
> muzyka krucha, nigdy nie powraca.
> Tam, w świata głuchych, wystygłych pałacach,
> donikąd wrócić nie będziesz się starał
> wiedząc, że słuszna nastąpiła kara
> za młodość bujną, sztukę wiarołomną.
>
> ("Dialog," *TZ*, 34)

> . . . And the art of throwing spells,
> a frail music, never comes back.
> There, in the world's castles, silent and grown cold
> you won't try to return to any place,
> knowing that you received a just punishment
> for your ardent youth, treacherous art.
>
> ("Dialogue," tr. E.M.)

How very small an offence seems the transgression of Czesław Miłosz, and yet the tone of censure sounds more than explicit. The dialogue between the Guide and the Pupil is not even a debating ground on which opposing but equal sides would clash, but a place in which an irresponsible and naive adept of art is given a raw reprimand not devoid of malicious overtones. Sometimes even virulent derision graces the words of the Guide. A modern Hamlet stooping over Yorick's skull is a distinctly grotesque figure. Vain reflection is totally foreign to him: the human skull, sleeping in ash, becomes simply the source of his aesthetic "rapture" and an additional source serving to sanction the need for an existence undefiled by the memory of death, a need which appears to the Pupil like "an eternal song, as long as I am light and movement." A person who hears in sacred music only the voice of romantic choirs, who hears the sound of bracelets in the knocking of a beggar's stick, does not deserve anything more than a word of derisive contempt. The conception of life as carefree joy and art, which "wiernie mi służy / i lekko biegnie za stukiem serca" (*TZ*, 33) ["it serves me faithfully / and runs lightly with a beat of the heart" (tr. A.R.)] is subjected here to a severe vivisection. The question posed by the Guide is a most instructive accusation:

> A w ręce, zżartej snami ziemskimi,
> co trzymasz? berło?
> Czy tylko świecę, błyszczącą podziemi
> martwym materiom?
>
> ("Dialog," *TZ*, 32)

> And in your hand, scalded by earthly dreams
> what do you hold? A sceptre?
> Or only a candle glowing under ground
> for lifeless things.
>
> ("Dialogue," tr. E.M.)

The poet's activity, or perhaps even his duty, is to sing the praises of life's charms and the beauties of the world, but his authorization ends when the vision becomes one-sided, and thereby mendacious. The reduction of the nature of human existence exclusively to terms of joy and Arcadian "singing" is a simplification which trivializes the genuine determinants of man's inscription in the world. Natural human joys obviously are counted as such determinants but at the same time eschatological questions are an inseparable component of man's fate both as individual and as species and through them he is brought face to face with death and eternity. The poet, who is the heir of the romantic bards and prophets, to whom is given the privilege of transcending with his gaze the universe of temporal reality, who is able to transcend the limits of personal existence and enter into the realm of the obsolete, has no right to give up his authorization under threat of artistic-moral banishment. An artist as an advocate of temporality is a figure as pitiful as Hamlet would have been if he had dug up the skull of his jester with the *haughty superiority of the living*. Art which chooses to concern itself exclusively with the transmaterial dimension is worthy of being condemned and despised since it forsakes the possibility of discovering in the transformations of history and the transience of human life some sort of higher order, a principle capable of defining and verifying the meaning of human action. A literature which sets as its sole aim to accompany concrete existence, to attest to the sudden whims and desires of the human herd irreversibly sets itself on the level of existence, and not beyond or above it. If literature's task is to declare itself on the side of those values which do not crumble with every turn of history, then it cannot permit itself to bend under the weight of concrete reality, to affirm that which is impermanent and transient, nor to revise the Decalogue according to the demands of a given epoch and its inhabitants. Its task is to declare itself on the side of a higher order of being.

> "Wawrzyn jest niedostępny nam, świadomym kary
> jaką czas tym wyznaczą, którzy pokochali
> doczesność, ogłuszoną hałasem metali"
>
> ("O książce," *TZ*, 22)

> Laurels are beyond our reach, we are aware of the punishment
> meted out by time to those who fell in love
> with temporality.
>
> ("On a Book," *WLA*, 413)

The urgency of this necessity grows in relation to the extent to which the world is ever increasingly branded with signs of the collapse of the hitherto reigning order of things, in relation to the increase in the number of cracks in the tissue of human existence. It is precisely time in which the impermanence of norms is made manifest, as is the fleeting nature of the principles which support social coexistence and the crisis-like character of a given cultural system and it is time which, in particular, requires an art which is capable of opposing the erosive processes which wear on human consciousness. Not submission to the mechanisms of temporality, but an appeal to an order which resists historical catastrophes can be the sole foundation of an art which does not wish to breathe its last along with its already expiring epoch. To this end there is need of a far-reaching revision and verification of truths which have hitherto constituted creative practices.

> . . . pora, żebyś ty powstał i biegł,
> chociaż ty nie wiesz, gdzie jest cel i brzeg,
> ty widzisz tylko, że ogień świat pali.
> I nienawidzieć pora co kochałeś,
> i kochać to, co znienawidziłeś,
> i twarze deptać tych, którzy milczącą
> piękność wybrali.
>
> ("Roki," *TZ*, 48)

> It's time for you to rise and to run
> though you don't know your goal and your end,

all you see is that fire burns the world,
and it's time to hate what once you loved,
to love what once you learned to hate.
And to tread on the faces of those who opted for
silent beauty.

("Assizes," tr. E.M.)

It is difficult not to ask if indeed the accusation which Miłosz directs against his poetry is truly that well founded. Were the sins of egoism, trusting in transitory temporality and being attuned to the joys of life really the transgression of his poetry? While reading the pages of *Poemat o czasie zastygłym* (Poem on Time Frozen) as well as the articles in *Żagary*, we are more likely to be convinced of something to the contrary. Indeed, his declaration on the side of the suffering mass, the slogans of social upheaval in the name of social justice, the insistent contrasting of images of vitalistic youth with visions of dying and human suffering, the search for a transhistorical perspective and the universalizing accents of his debut collection are able to create a satisfactory defense in the face of such a classification. Of course, certain egotistical longings of Miłosz are discernible in this collection. His articles published towards the end of the 1930s reveal the compulsion to which the poet submitted himself under the heading of "social" therapy, nevertheless this material is too scanty to form a basis upon which such strong accusation could be formulated. It is more appropriate to assume that the prosecutorial tone of the poet is more probably a result of that which was hidden from the eyes of the reader, than of that which may be an artistic document with a questionable basis.

The visions of collective experience outlined in his "social" poems and in several of his programmatic articles dispose the reader towards a moment of reflection. There was very little room in them for the consideration of questions of ethics, metaphysics or the transcendental aspirations of man. Visions of the culture of a world of "free producers" led in general to a perspective of satisfaction of the most basic needs of man, while remaining silent regarding his "higher" needs for fulfillment. This world of "tomorrow" was to be forced upon him in the form of psychological coercion. And so, therefore, the individual could not become a *co-determinant* of the above-mentioned prognosticated reality, but received it in that form which the official mandarins of historical transformation had considered the only appropriate one. In this plan we actually do encounter a situation which, speaking with his strangely Maritain-like voice, the Guide would not be able to accept. The social poet of *Żagary* certainly was expected to declare himself on the side of "matter" against the spiritual order. He was expected to, but in point of fact he never did definitely declare himself on the side of those who held in their hand "the candle which lights the dead matter of the underground." We can say, therefore, that the dispute concerning the artistic ethics of the writer does not have a particular person as addressee in the same way that Maritain's *Art et Scolastique* (*Art and Wisdom*) has no such addressee. "Dialog" is a discourse on the subject of the contemporary tasks of poetry and a polemic with all those who treat art exclusively as a ludificative activity, turning away from the world of eschatological realizations and forgetting about the moral calling of the artist.

We remember, after all, what Maritain, the author of *Humanisme intégral (An Integral Humanism)*, said: Art should be an act of moral heroism and internal discipline, joining within itself the aesthetic with the ethical, and thereby guaranteeing the writer a sense of creative freedom, reminding him at the same time of his obligation to accompany his fellow man. These postulates are not easily followed in the practice of art. They inform, in a very general way, what the duties and obligations of the artist are. However, they are not able to provide answers to specific questions. From them it is not possible to find out how far the independence of the poet reaches or at what point it must be curbed; it can give no answer to the question by what methods and means is it possible to maintain ties with the modern day Sisyphus or to the question to what extent art should be determined by the demands of its epoch or how necessary it is to go beyond its own "time-node." Maritain's conceptions, despite all their unquestionable value, are still conceptions of a "golden mean." They join within themselves opposing sets of artistic directives together with their ethical conditions, stressing the "importance" of the mutually opposed elements, opting for the kind of system of laws and obligations governing the artist which would, within the framework of a concrete cultural model, soothe the antinomy between a world torn by contradictions and the artist who, despite being equally ambivalent internally, is trying to integrate it.

Truly great art is invariably based in a tragic consciousness, which obliges the artist to absolutize certain values at the expense of the others, and forces him to choose between contradictory sets of humanistic values. It is always accompanied by indecision and perplexity. The proposition of the French philosopher rests on an attempt to place the artist at such a point where he will not have to choose between alternatives, but instead would have the opportunity to harmoniously join opposites. In the sphere of theoretical considerations where, in the most general manner, a set of artistic aims is formulated and the image of the world is disantagonized within the limits of an imagined aesthetic postulate, it is possible to build such an absolutist model. It is otherwise, however, when, encircled by the antinomies of reality, limited by the possibilities of his own imagination and his own creative workshop, put at the mercy of the events and phenomena which obscure the contours of the world, the artist must, with practically every line of every poem, with every metaphor or image, repeatedly renew that choice. Just as knowledge of the code of ethical norms is in no way a guarantee to the individual of a just life, so a personal appropriation of Maritain's artistic decalogue is not able to save the artist from straying in the thicket of possibilities and aesthetic tactics. Miłosz, therefore, creates a situation in which his poetry will be able to be located at the intersection of those resultants which tear the tissue of reality and those forces which push the artist towards mutually incompatible creative decisions. How to create poetry which will at one and the same time be a flash of a world-building imagination but not break away from real existence? How to create a situation in which the poet guarantees himself independence in relation to artistic and world view strategies, yet still does not break the ties joining him to the collective? How to maintain an individual perspective while simultaneously transforming the feelings of people in general? What sort of form of artistic communication to choose, such that it would be deeply rooted in its own epoch but at the same time would treat universal questions? How to distance oneself from a consciousness which is a product of concrete conditions of society and civilization but not become, at the same time, an inspired Cassandra whose words no one will be able to believe? How to declare oneself on the side of the axiological constants of human culture, but still not repudiate those values which determine the artist's attachment to a specific world?

These questions could be multiplied almost endlessly, encompassing ever newer areas of phenomena and problems. The drastic contradictoriness of the intentions which are beginning, at this point, to guide the way for Miłosz seems to be whispering that to set out on the road trodden by the thought of Catholic personalism is to threaten the artist with defeat by eclecticism. How, therefore, can one practice an art which is at once both "pure" and "applied," how can one speak in one's own voice but also that of others, how can one remain true to the "spiritual" order without turning away from "matter?" A poet who has his gaze fixed on noble ethical ideals such as patronizing a truly humanistic art, an art which simply cannot agree with the repudiation of any values whatsoever, finds himself in an unusually difficult situation. His attempt, if it is not to be defeated by the impotence of eclecticism, must at this point become an attempt at the impossible, a dramatic search for an artistic absolute.

Let us not forget that we are dealing with a writer who, with his very first volume, set out on a tightrope journey through a world of antinomies. Even the first poem referred to herein from the volume *Trzy zimy* was an attempt to cross certain barriers which seem to separate the prophetic vision from a lyrical "*reportage.*" An imaginative document of the experience of the tragic nature of the epoch to which it belongs from the "account" of an observer of history, which separates a concrete description of nature from an apocalyptic vision of a disintegrating cosmos. By what stratagem does Miłosz elect to deal with this most difficult situation? How does he intend to extricate himself from the tangle of impossibilities bearing in upon him from all sides? Where will he seek salvation for his tragic individual?

Stefan Napierski was one of very few critics from the interwar period who was able to discern in Miłosz's *Trzy zimy* something more than just a flood of expressive images which repel any attempt to intellectually dehermeticize them as well as a totally and simply black picture of the approaching historical conflagration. He perceived a great deal more, it seems, and although he did not choose to derive more extensive conclusions from his perceptions, nevertheless he accurately identified the main lines of the thematic-problematic tension which permeates these poems.

In his review on the pages of *Ateneum*, he wrote:

> This poet, whose longer poems, in particular, whirl chaotically, if not to say monstrously, and are bent by the weight of bewitchingly rich circumlocutions, has astoundingly homogeneous, almost simplistic, mental raw material, and this joins him to his generation. Like all of them, he is unable to integrate himself, he stands immobilized over his own abyss, discerning monsters where there is only the whirling of youth to which it befell to grow up in an epoch out of harmony with its bases. Practically all of his poems, in great poetic magic and dazzling beauty grow out of the landscape which he shared with his compatriot Mickiewicz, landscapes of Belorussian lakes, Orthodox churches, half pagan wilderness and half legendary steppes of hunters, and with the greatest difficulty, through a tangle of expressions, move towards the myth

> which, in the face of the seduction and pathos of annihilation, is to save and consolidate this natural "land of childhood," their native landscape of the spirit.[3]

The author of *Rozmowy z cieniem* (Conversation with a Shadow) has, in this only apparently chaotic fragment, very skillfully reconstructed the network of internal oppositions, and frequently at the same time implications, developed on the pages of *Trzy zimy*. The expansion of the formally imaginative-symbolic visions but, to no less an extent, the simplicity of the conceptual principles governing this vortex of images; the integral pessimism of the creator-subject, but at the same time his immediate ties with the tragic dilemmas of an epoch cracking at its foundations; sensuous and concrete scenes of nature yet equally its precise link with the romantic tradition; the "landscape" of destruction but to an equal extent its mythical structure and function; the freedom of poetic expression but also its discrete functionalization within the limits of the described network of mutual interdependences—these would seem to form the fundamental set of lines which can be extracted from the pages of this volume. But there is still one more: the unfailing presence of the two constant clichés of recognition and vision, and of the concrete and myth. Juxtaposed to each other, ever penetrating and opalizing, they create a totally unique image of the world which, being strongly rooted in the reality of nature and society-civilization, is simultaneously a construction which is its own interpretation. *Trzy zimy* is not only a poetic diagnosis of reality, but also a proposal for a certain understanding of it, such a reading as would—through a set of mythical structures—justify, explain and visualize its internal image. If it is true, as A. Fiut writes, that "the main function of myth is consequently to give meaning to reality and to human existence"[4] and if, in essence, its task is to organize notions of the world in such a way that by reference to the sphere of transrational reasons and the delineation of an alternative strategy of the world, then it becomes a definite interpretation of a world which is difficult to accept, and it is difficult, in the flood of catastrophic images of Miłosz's second volume not to discover this cognitive-therapeutic design. "Apocalypse," "Nature," "Prophecy,"—these are essentially the three problematic keys which open before us in this poetic book. However, they open it completely only when we are willing to see, in their presence, not only a replica of social reality or an attempt at self-liberation from its pressure—through an escape into the hermetic world of metaphors and accumulated levels of images,—but equally a timid design of the sort of model of the universe which it would reveal by its very own hidden "logic."

If one were to look at Miłosz's interwar poems, i.e., those written after 1933, from the perspective of the pessimistic diagnoses arising directly out of the analysis of socio-political reality, then one would be met by a certain disenchantment. Contrary to our expectations, we will not find many distinctions which we could tie in directly to the realities of the interwar period. One of the most eagerly summoned images of catastrophe is from the well-known "Bramy arsenału" ("The Gates of the Arsenal"):

> Suknie spadną zetlałe, krzak włosów zgoreje
> i brzuch goły odsłoni jak koło z mosiądzu,
> uda ruchliwe odtąd marzeniem nie rządzą,
> nagie i czyste dymią jak rude Pompeje.
>
> A jeśli dziecko zrodzi się z tej krwi słowiańskiej,
> patrząc bielmem, łbem ciężkim na stopnie potoczy
> i z czworgiem łap w powietrzu w dzień będzie i w nocy
> spać, jak koń martwy w runi wypalonych pastwisk.
>
> ("Bramy arsenału," *TZ,* 13—14)

> Her dress will fall off in flames, the bush of hair will blaze
> And reveal her belly like a copper disk.
> Her nimble thighs no more rule over dreams,
> Naked and pure they smoke like red Pompei.
>
> And if a child is born of that Slavic blood,
> White-eyed, it will strike its head hard against the steps
> And sleep with its four legs up, day and night
> As a dead horse sleeps amid burnt-out pastures.
>
> ("The Gates of the Arsenal," *CP,* 11)

As concerns the diagnostic value of this fragment, which carries one of the more frequently displayed of the numerous interpretations of the lyrical poetry produced by the vision of the Żagary group, it is necessary to admit that its appearance in the work is somewhat unexpected. The gloomy atmosphere of strolls through Łazienki Park, amidst the monuments and scenery which evoke associations with the tragic peripeties of Polish insurrectional martyrology, is formed by the restless projections of a surrealistic imagination which are superimposed as a mobile mosaic of shapes, lights and shadows on the realistically static park, where gravel crunches under the foot of a pedestrian, lovers sit down on the steps by the water which is carrying off a sailboat released by children, and "families of dogs" chase through the flowerbeds, and is then suddenly completed by a piercing radiation of light from which "all that is alive dies."

If Miłosz had written this work at least ten years later, after the atomic experiments at Hiroshima and Nagasaki, it would not be difficult for us to interpret the vision and the genetic effects of radiation disease. However, the awareness of the location of this work in the mid-1930s forces us to situate it amidst the visions which derive their inspiration from the apocalyptic tradition of the Bible. The union of surrealistic depictions with eschatological imaginings frequently produces totally surprising effects in the lyrical poetry of the Żagarist.

From where, then, can we derive the presence of this work of this startling vision of biological destruction which strikes the entities which are given up to it as prey and causes the degeneration of subsequent generations? It is apparently not accidental that in this work Miłosz so expressly stresses the presence of the historical background which incessantly accompanies the individual who is in contact with this seemingly Arcadian garden. Its discrete but undeniable presence forms an unceasing reminder of man's temporal determination. Walking amongst the statues is a historical repetition, a resurrection amongst those who have been magically contained in the stone of the monuments and those who performed *the feat of immortalization.*[5] The present day is not an oasis in the flowing stream of time. It is equally subject to the annihilating force of time's current, and it can also come to experience historical destruction. The boys setting tin soldiers on the toy sailboat have the same chance of escaping the reach of the burning "ray of death" as did the previous generation. The inertia and immobility of reality is only apparent, the foot moving along the gravel "treads in a false calmness," "the blowing of the wind from the abyss" indicates history is beginning to respire, a renewed liberation of the winds of history, which are to blow over a congealed Eden. This world is situated between fall and winter, dusk and night, silence and noise, between fair weather and a rising storm; even dream—"the garden of madness"—only appears to be a shelter for existence which is essentially "a handful of ash."

> Reality has no nooks into which we can escape from our transitoriness. We are condemned to existence in time. Miłosz tries to revoke that condition. It is possible to depart into dream, which is a special sort of distension of time, a freezing of transitoriness. However, every total act of

> acceptance of dream is equivalent to a repetition of the waking state. . . . When we step across the threshold of dream we enter into another time and each of our covenants with dream must end with the extinguishing of the flame of our time. This "dream-entry" is . . . an entering into timelessness, a union of our transitory nature with divine unchangingness. And that is why we perish, because our life is based on change, while our immortality is equivalent to the lack of change which, however you look at it, means death.[6]

Miłosz himself does not treat this dream-like immortality completely seriously, realizing that this escape can last as long as it takes for the sun to complete an orbit on the firmament ("for a short time, as long as the sun's flight, take it"). A union with a dream "power" is an extemporaneous pact, only apparently promising man an escape from the rule of temporal laws. Presence in time—historical and biological—means submission to its destructive claims, means recognition of the laws of History and of the Cosmos.

An equally frequently summoned image, intended to justify the directly understood catastrophism of this collection, is the following fragment:

> Zamknij okno, tam idą germańskie Junony
> I skaczą w moje rzeki, senne tonie burzą,
> Gdzie przedtem tylko rybak nad siecią niedużą
> Stał w czajek i jaskółek goniącym się kole.
> Czarne, wojenne wozy zorały pastwiska,
> Lecą ognie chorągwi, aż czerwono błyaska
> Ściana nad łóżkiem, szklanki dygocąa na stole.
>
> ("Fragment," *W* (1967), 30)

> Close the window, German women, each like Juno,
> march there, jump into my rivers, disturb sleepy waters,
> where before only a fisherman above his small net
> stood in a circle of darting lapwings and swallows.
> Black war chariots furrowed my pastures,
> flames of banners fly by, a red glow flickers
> on a wall above my bed, cups shake on the table.
>
> ("Fragment," tr. E.M.)

This work also, contrary to appearances, does not provide us with much opportunity to treat it as a poetic analysis of concrete historical reality.

"Germańskie *Junony*," "military carts" and trembling walls of the hospital are all fairly general war-related signs. "Germańskie Junony" [or "German women, like Juno," as translated by Cz. Miłosz] are youths with swastikas on their sleeves, but equally it could be Wichman or Gero; "military carts" certainly means tanks, but also chariots or other military vehicles. Very rarely in his creative works does Miłosz, right up until today, ever become seduced by the material phenomenality of his epoch. He always seeks out those signs which refer him to concrete reality but which, at the same time, have inscribed in them a certain transtemporal quality. Even such an apparently realistic work as "O książce" ("On a Book") employs a "lens" which universalizes a so contemporary military threat:

W czasach dziwnych i wrogich żyliśmy, wspaniałych,
nad głowami naszemi pociski śpiewały
i lata niemniej groźne od rwących szrapneli
nauczały wielkości tych co nie widzieli
wojny. W pożarze sucho płonących tygodni
pracowaliśmy ciężko i byliśmy głodni
chleba, cudów nieziemskich zjawionych na ziemi
i często, spać nie mogąc, nagle zasmuceni
patrzyliśmy przez okna, czy nad noce sine
nie przypływają stada zeppelinów
czy nie wybucha sygnał nowy kontynentom
i sprawdzaliśmy w lustrze, czy na czole piętno
nie wyrosło, na znak, żeśmy już skazani.
. . . .
była epoka burzy, dzień apokalipsy,
państwa dawne zburzono, stolice wrzecionem
kręciły się pijane pod niebem spienionem.

("O książce," *TZ*, 21)

We lived in strange and horrible, stupendous times,
over our heads artillery shells were singing,
and years no less threatening than shrapnels
taught greatness to those who have not seen
war. In the fire of weeks burning dry
we worked hard and were hungry
for bread and for unearthly miracles on earth,

and often, grieving, unable to sleep
we looked at the windows to make certain
that flocks of Zeppelins don't invade the blue night,
that a new signal for the continents
does not burst forth as yet.
And we checked in the mirrors whether a mark
on our foreheads did not announce that we were doomed.
. . . .
It was the time of tempest, day of the Apocalypse,
old States lay in ruins, capitals spinned,
drunk, under a foaming sky.

("On a Book," tr. E.M.)

The historical turmoil whose inevitability Miłosz proclaims in his works, will become an event in terms of its cruelty *sui generis,* but will be, at the same time, a repetition of an age-old pattern known to man for centuries. The scenery of the events will change, the actors of the military events who exit into nothingness will change, but nevertheless "pod tym samym nieuchronnym / asyryjskim, egipskim i rzymskin /księżycem" ("Hymn," *TZ,* 16) ["under the same immobile / Assyrian, Egyptian, and Roman / moon" ("Hymn," *CP,* 14)] the same, though contemporary, drama will be played out. The lands on the banks of the Vistula or the Somme are simply the sites of the "modern Troy"; the destroyed European metropolises hiss in the fire the same way as "the burnt palaces of King Balthazar"; the annihilation of contemporary civilization will be added as one more page in the Book of Historical Apocalypse.

Both "Fragment" and "O książce" are basically concerned with the same thing, i.e., with the illusory nature of Arcadia, in which man seeks refuge from the inferno of catastrophic realizations. Neither *locus amoenus* on the banks of the Vilia nor the world of cultural "gardens" is a refuge for man. Natural "groves" will be ploughed and rutted by the war machines while the works of Conrad and Norwid will turn out to be out-of-date in the face of the new "laws of history, which will be veiled by a red dust storm." The catastrophe is irreversible and there is no means by which to alter the course of events which is drawing humanity nearer to its tragic end.

Ni zapomnieniem wiecznym, ani pamiętaniem,
mgłą gór, ni stolic wrzawą świat nie uspokoi.

Aż po latach bojowań krzyż albo i kamień,
i ptak zaśpiewa na nim, jak w ruinach Troi.
("Elegia," *TZ*, 18)

Not with eternal oblivion, nor with remembering,
not with mountain mist, nor the din of big cities
will the world calm you. After years of battling
you will get a cross or a stone, and on it
a bird will sing as on the ruins of Troy.
("Elegy," *WLA*, 421)

Yet from where does this inflexible certainly of the inevitability of the Apocalypse derive? If Miłosz in his poems, does not derive it from definite political circumstances, then it might seem possible that the consciousness of the destructiveness of the actions of history would be very easily pushed aside by the vitality of one's own existence. Yet this consciousness does not give such a certainty either.

Oto wędrujamy przez wieki, mordując, paląc i niszcząc.
Oto budujemy miasta, aby obrócić w popioły.
Rodzą się nam dzieci złością napojone i w kołysce sięgają po nóż,
pierwszą zabawą ich kamień, radością nienawiść dla słabych.
("Brama wieczoru")[7]

Here we are: wandering throughout ages,
  murdering, burning and destroying.
Here we are: building cities and turning them into ashes.
Children are born filled with anger and in the cradle reaching out for
  a knife
and their first toy is a stone, and their joy is the hatred of those who
  are weak.
("The Gate of Evening," tr. E.M.)

Death, destruction and hatred are the norms of human existence, and there is no reason to suppose that the present age will prove to be free from the same fate. Quite the opposite, as one look at the surrounding world convinces him that the time of the next conflagration has arrived. In "Wiersze" ("Poems") he states: "Piekła żądałeś? Oto się odsłania, więc patrz uważnie . . ." ["You wanted hell? Here it is revealing itself, so look closely . . ." (tr. A.R.)].[8]

Signs of the menace are coming from all sides. The world of nature congeals under the poetic eye in hideous and repulsive shapes and appears most often as a bare, burnt to ashes desert, overgrown with astounding plants:

> Pod rozpalonym słońcem milczenie popiołów.
>
> ("Ptaki," *TZ*, 5)

> Under the burning-hot sun the silence of ashes.
>
> ("Birds," tr. A.R.)

> Najzieleńsze drzewa jak ołów rozkwitły w środku nocy.
>
> ("Hymn," *TZ*, 25)

> The greenest of trees like lead blooming in the midst of the night.
>
> ("Hymn," *CP*, 13)

> Wszystko minione, wsystko zapomniane,
> Tylko na ziemi dym, umarłe chmury,
> i nad rzekami z popiołu tlejące
> skrzydła i cofa się zatrute słońce,
> a potępienia brzask wychodzi z mórz.
>
> ("Roki," *TZ*, 48)

> Everything has passed, everything is forgotten,
> only smoke upon the earth, dead clouds
> over the rivers of ashes, smoldering wings,
> and the poisoned sun retreats,
> and the dawn of damnation rises from the seas.
>
> ("Assizes," tr. E.M.)

This is the landscape of a world which for a long time has been ripe for Apocalypse. Every effort undertaken to save the collapsing order is condemned from the outset to failure. Every human action is sterile and only hastens the process of general entropy. Above the world whose end is drawing near, mysterious forces are assuming power and controlling even the hand of man:

> Jeżeli jestem rolnikiem, ty rękami moimi pracujesz nad zniszczeniem
> traw rozpiętych w ugorach i osuszasz błota,

aż wyrastają płody i wódka narodom spragnionym
jak manna spływa kroplami w pokorne gardła.
("Hymn," *TZ*, 17)

If I am a farmer, you are using my hands
to destroy grasses spreading on fallows, and I drain marshes
till you can harvest, and thirsty nations
receive manna, drops of vodka, into their humbled throats.
("Hymn," tr. E.M.)

The image of reality which Miłosz has constructed in *Trzy zimy* shocks us by its uncompromising extremism. On the one hand, naked and scorched earth, and on the other the silence of the "spheres" which appear to have been abandoned in resignation by the Demiurge, who has given everything up as plunder to Satan who is leading man to the last circle of Hell. A world deprived of any transcendent support become a field of total collapse in which any values, norms or principles whatsoever cease to exist. It is lacking in a foundation on which it would be possible to base an effort at transformation. Herling-Grudziński's assertion was correct when he wrote:

> the first strong and suggestive vision which the poet achieved, being entangled in human affairs, submerged in them,—he himself human, walking the earth—was to see the earth destroyed, demolished, in ruins, as after a fire or a flood. The first circle of Hell, for which he wished to depart in his eschatological journey, was to be the earth itself: denuded, black, pinkened by a red glow and visited by solitarily floating flocks of birds which are flying away from people.[9]

In this situation it is difficult not to ask how the poet in his works imagined the world of man. Does it also totally become the same kind of charred or burnt-out ruin? Already the first work of this collection implies the announcement of a complete answer:

Czem jestem, czem ja jestem i czem oni są?
Upici kwaśnem winem, czerwone wypieki
zakrywają i rzędem nad brzegami śpią.

. . . .
Słychać z dna białych jarów dzwoneczki kuglarza.

Trąbka gra. Dźwięk przerażeń śpiące ziemie budzi,
("Ptaki," *TZ*, 5–6)

What am I, what am I and what are they?
Drunken with sour wine, covering their flashed cheeks,
they sleep in a row by the riverside.

. . . .

From the bottom of white canyons a juggler's little bells
are heard. A trumpet calls. The sound of terrors wakes the sleeping lands,
("Birds," tr. E.M.)

The human universe, like the world of nature is subject to the process of disintegration which transforms individuals into a herd vainly striving to forget about death. "Man is given to the earth only, let him desire no other"— says the choir to Anna in "Pieśń" ("Song" [*SN*, 91]). This is a central and fundamental truth which accompanies all of the lyrical heroes of this collection. Nothing at all is able to soothe the memory of it. Already in *Poemat o czasie zastygłym* (Poem on Time Frozen) Miłosz had continually brought together images of human beauty and youth, in order to shatter them with dramatic conclusions about vanity, in order to complete them with visions of disintegration and death filled with suffering. In *Trzy zimy* he moves even further. Even the bonds of feelings in which man takes refuge before the threat of a world shocking in its nihilism are only an alliance in anticipation of that which alone is certain and ineluctable.

I tak oboje będziemy czekali
Na promień ostry, który nas otwiera,
Nie wiem, czy gdy się żyje, czy umiera.
("Postój zimowy," *O*, 62)

And thus we both shall wait
for something to open us, a piercing ray,
when, I don't know, while living or dying.
("Winter Halt," tr. E.M.)

czuję twój dotyk jeszcze, twój dotyk szyję mnie pali.
Noce miłosne z tobą gorzkie jak popiół chmur,
("Pieśń, *TZ*, 10)

Your touch burns my neck. I still feel it.
Nights of love bitter as ash from the clouds,

("Song," *SN*, 93)

Love, physical union and eroticism are supposed to grant protection from the consciousness of doom but emphasize even more the finitude of this momentary existence, and even more dramatically restore man "to the earth." A. Fiut writes:

> love is for Miłosz, above all, an act of physical union. It is a temptation—sinful—to separation from the enigmas of the world and renewed submersion in unconsciousness, in a state of vegetative inert existence. It is a temptation to seek refuge from the pressure of a hostile reality—in the maternal womb. However, the love act does not bring alleviation. On the contrary, after a momentary intoxication there follows an ever so unpleasant awakening. . . . The poet is more inclined to associate the erotic with suffering and pain than with pleasure and joy, and contact with a woman does not satisfy the hunger for truth and does not placate metaphysical nostalgia.[10]

Human life is unceasing anticipation of the arrival of death. Each passing day, each new wrinkle on our skin, is a reminder of the absurdity which is our brief existence, which we spend anxiously and intently gazing at the signs of time carving ruts on our incessantly aging faces.

Ona wstaje ze zmiętej pościeli.
O sukniach i podróżach w swoich snach myślała.
Przed czarne lustro idzie. Młodość krótko trwała,
. . . .
Uda zasłonić, niech nie wspominają
kłębami cienkich fioletowych żył:
. . . .
Przed lustrem nago stojąc dwie łzy
lekko wyciera kobieta chusteczką
i farbą przyciemnia brew.

("Świty," *TZ*, 23–24)

She gets up from her crumpled sheets.
In her dreams she thought of dresses and travel.
She walks up to the black mirror. Youth didn't last long.

. . . .
To cover up one's thighs. Let them not,
With their lacing of thin purple veins, remember
. . . .
Standing naked in front of her mirror, the woman
Lightly wipes away a couple of tears with her kerchief
And darkens her eyebrows with henna.

("Dawns," *CP*, 17)

It is not by chance that, in his argument with the priest, Fr. Ch., Miłosz ultimately admits the other is right. It is precisely this prematurely wizened fanatic, burning with hatred of "the wedding of bodies," and knowing "that from human happiness, not a stone will remain standing," who is, in the final accounting, right. Everything which is material and subject to the flow of time will sooner or later suffer disintegration.

. . . Od jego to siły
w pył, w szarej ziemi urodzajne iły
zmienia się ciało umierając długo,
a umysł gorzkim poddawany próbom,
błądzi, straciwszy miłość swą na wieki.
Żal, smutek czasu przestrzeni dalekich
szumią w tym kraju. Wicher włosy siwe
czesze palcami i wreszcie prawdziwe
słowa powtarza wpatrzonym w pamięci
przzapaść otwartą.

("Dialog," *TZ*, 33–34)

. . . Under its power
the body, slowly dying, changes
into dust and fertile loams of earth,
while the mind, put to bitter tests,
wander, having lost its love for ever.
Grief, sadness of time's remote spaces
roar in this land. The gale with its fingers
combs grey hair and repeats at last
words of truth to those who stare
into an open chasm of memory.

("Dialogue," tr. E.M.)

And yet it is difficult not to observe that, parallel to these images of complete doubt and the total negation of the value of life, Miłosz, unceasingly and time and again anew, faces this problem, and in the sphere of these very same qualities which he had so definitively questioned, he seeks strengthening consolation. Henryk Vogler asserts that such a construction is not accidental, that within the poet there is a struggle between "attachment to the earth, a desire for corporeality, a striving towards a totality of life's experience and a hopeless disbelief in the truth of this earthliness and a desire to attain higher nonmaterial forms of existence."[11] Essentially, therefore, death and disintegration belong to the same order of things as life, eroticism and sensual pleasure. Having reached the limit beyond which there is now only the disintegration of the world and the stars falling from the firmament to earth, flocks of zeppelins flying up to the windows and earth scorched to its clay, and also slowly decomposing disintegration as the limits of human existence, the poet springs up as if to a renewed effort. Having destroyed the earth which had been struck by the wing of the apocalypse and having stripped humanity of its last hope, he begins a heroic journey to a brighter horizon. Writing of Miłosz's searchings and indicating the inhuman character of such an experiment Herling-Grudziński adds in conclusion:

> The journeys of poets are not infrequently attended by misunderstanding. After all, if someone, out of concern for man, destroys his evil Earth in order to sail on a black ship to the beginning of the creation of everything, that is not, as some would have it, a sick prophet or a false bombaster, but a symptom of the humanism of our times.[12]

An attempt to see the apocalypse as humanism?—that is indeed an interesting perspective. Miłosz's poetry of the interwar period is an attempt to attain to that point beyond which there is nothing, the boundary which must give birth to a rebellion against the senselessness of existence and the satanocratic vision of the world. The poet writes in "Świty":

> Za mało. Życia jednego za mało.
> Dwa razy żyć chciałbym na smutnej planecie,
> w miastach samotnych, we wsiach pełnych głodu,
> patrzeć na wszelkie zło, na rozpad ciał,
> i prawa zbadać, którym był podległy
> czas, co nad nami jak wiatr ze świstem wiał.
>
> ("Świty," *TZ*, 23)

Not enough. One life is not enough.
I'd like to live twice on this sad planet,
In lonely cities, in starved villages,
To look at all evil, at the decay of bodies,
and probe the laws to which time was subject,
time that howled above us like a wind.

("Dawns," *CP*, 16)

"It seems," says Napierski, "that Miłosz, even though such a young artist [. . .] came to a halt at the ghostly point from which he had set out on his earthly journey at the edge of the 'sea of nothingness': and that shore is, as it were, once again, the threshold of belief."[13] If we are, in actuality, to understand catastrophism as a world view which develops visions of annihilation while seeking ways to save humanistic values, then without a doubt we will discover here the poetry of the author of "Hymn." The development of a pessimistic perspective and looking at the world from a distance outside of history seem to serve a specific cognition. We must understand this historicity in a rather specific sense, because Miłosz is not like the historical researcher who juxtaposes past events seeking out their identity with each other in their structural organization. His reflections on the cruelty of history and its laws have the character of the most general sorts of reflections which are far from any notion of precision whatsoever. "Under 'historicity,'" writes Błoński, "the poet does not understand either the present or the laws which history obeys. It is something more like the substance of the experience of humanity . . ."[14] However, that experience suggests to the artist that no historical disaster has the quality of finality, that destruction is answered by the construction which subsequently ensues, likewise demolition is answered by erection, and collapse by the arduous raising up of the over-strained "house of man" i.e., humanity. That is not, however, how a consistent catastrophist would express himself, because for him the dehumanization of the world is always an irreversible process. That is, indubitably, how an eschatologist would express himself, seeing in the fulfillment of prophetic auguries the approach of the day of restitution. It is precisely this sort of conviction that can be heard in Miłosz's poetry:

Cóż by zostało z nas, gdyby odjąć ten głód ugięcia kolan
i zachwycenie, co plamę okrucieństwa zwycięża,
cóż by nas uratować mogło, gdybyśmy nie doznali
spojrzenia, które skały naszego życia otwiera?

Domie kruchy sekund prawdziwych,
znaku żywych pośrodku nas żywych
czym byśmy wtedy byli, gdyby miłość nas nie ogarnęła?
("Brama wieczoru")[15]

What would remain of us without our desire to bend our knees,
and the enchantment that overcomes the stain of cruelty.
What would save us, if we did not know
the glance that opens the rocks of our lives?
O frail house of seconds become real,
o sign of life among us who are alive!
What would we become, if not engulfed by love?
("The Gate of Evening," tr. E.M.)

And therefore, this knowledge indicates a search for a transcendental foundation on which it would be possible to lean in an infernal world. All the while, however, we remain in the sphere of those same values whose transience and menace the poet has suggested: love, affection, enchantment with the beauty of the world, and the hunger for metaphysics. There, however, they seemed to be embodied incompletely, not supported by the divine principle, while here they appear rooted in the transcendent and made sacred by a divine principle. Fiut was correct, then, when he wrote, rejecting axiological dualism in the case of Miłosz's poetry, that "he announces the destruction of all values and all of humanity. For this reason, the values which appear in his poetry do not lend themselves to organization according to two opposing systems—on the one hand life, youth, goodness, trust, ideal love, humility and beauty; on the other death, age, evil, falsity, sensual love and pride. Miłosz's axiological system is therefore a monistic system. Only one kind of values exists—universal and eternal. Any opposition would mean their degradation or imply contradictory anti-values."[16] Witkacy's catastrophism assumed the substitution of specified values by surrogate, apparent qualities. Miłosz's catastrophism still revolves in the sphere of those same values which, having been negated and rejected by the apostatic human collective, will be returned to the original incarnations. As such, which is characteristic, this catastrophism does not assume the total rejection of life as duration through time or of love as a sinful carnal act, but seeks for them a metaphysical justification. The return of the world to the channel of idealistic realizations is possible, however, only upon execution of the verdict of history. We remain, therefore, in the sphere of the biblical apocalypse, which maintained the necessity of the destructive world, which is in the hands of Satan and sin. The judgement which will liberate the small number of just men from the oppression of the forces of darkness and which will separate Good from Evil, darkness from light, injustice from justice, will become the eschatological stage embodying the new world of absolute actualizations. The destruction and razing of reality, and through that the annulment of the authority of the evil powers which hold it in their cruel care, are necessary, so that "a world such as it was in the beginning" can come to be. The fulfillment of destiny means a return to the beginning of Time, to a Paradise which is a garden of life.

Wychodzimy naprzeciw siebie i widzimy naszą słabą nagość,
wiecznie piękni i młodzi, wiecznie sprawiedliwi,
skaza, co była w nas, nie jest naszą istotą,
wszystko już zapomniane, tylko radość nie została zapomniana.
Stado mężczyzn i kobiet wiecujących po zmartwychwstaniu,
gdziekolwiek spojrzeć nadchodzą w tę dolinę niesłyszanych fraz
  muzycznych,
jedno dla drugiego ma miłość, jakiej dotychczas nie znali
  kochankowie,
miłość tak wielką, że nie pragnie nasycenia.
I dotykają do siebie z takim drżeniem zachwytu
i otulają rękami piersi małe i ostre,
nie po to, aby budzić pożądanie,
ale z samej radości, że tu w braterstwie żyją,
że są, że wszystko jest, czegokolwiek tak długo wyglądali.
("Brama wieczoru")

We move forward towards each other and see our nudity.
Forever beautiful and young, forever just,
the stigma we bore is not of our essence,
everything is forgotten, only joy has not been forgotten.
Flocks of men and women congregating after resurrection,
wherever you look, they arrive to this valley of wondrous musical
  phrases,
they have for each other love hitherto unknown to lovers,
love so strong that it does not desire fulfillment.
And they touch each other with such a trembling of delight

and with their hands they enfold tiny and pointed breasts,
not to evoke lust
but out of sheer joy that they live here in brotherhood,
that they exist, that everything they sought so long is here.
("The Gate of Evening," tr. E.M.)

Therefore, the shock into which man, condemned to annihilation, has been thrown, is the shock only of those who have the shame of transgression and those who were not given the light of knowledge. This is because the eschatological interpretation of the history of humanity discovers a Demiurge in compliance with a cosmic catastrophe which is to purge the world from wrongs, sin and the collapse of the Decalogue. The perspective opened up by Miłosz's eschatological catastrophism is a thoroughly optimistic prognosis,—it sacralizes human history. It is a voyage of humanity from the abyss of doubt into a transcendent dimension. At the foundation of the poet's reflections is the idea of the Eternal Return, achieved by the destruction of the world which is unable by itself to return to its original tracks. Through the darkness of the approaching annihilation, the outlines of this absolutist order are already shining through:

Na ten nowy ład
form odrodzonych, wyrażających chciwie
prawdę, od której lądy winny drżec, a ona
nadchodzi cicho i wieczór nie jest już wieczorem,
i ciężar nie jest już ciężarem,
i los nie jest już tym samym losem.
Bo oto spada błysk i ziemski dom rozdziela:
dobro jest tu i zło jest tu. I czeka nieśmiertelność.
("Dytyramb")[17]

. . . a new ordering
of forms reborn, expressing avidly
the truth that should make continents tremble
it arrives silently and the evening is not an evening anymore
and the burden ceases to be a burden
and fate is not the same fate.
For now a flame descends and cleaves the earthy house:
Good is here and evil is here. And immortality is given.
("Dithyramb," tr. E.M.)

S. Napierski, in the conclusion of his essay on *Trzy zimy*, wrote that "this classic, entwined in phantasmagoria, does not choose to be devoured by an enormous longing for exculpation."[18] Not perceiving, in the flood of overlapping layers of images and visions, the outlines of the eschatological vision of the world which, despite everything, affirms the meaningfulness of the history of humanity amidst events seemingly torn apart from transcendent supervision, he does however, see the great hunger for order and morality, the longing for the rebuilding of the hierarchy of the world, and the anticipation of the shock which could reestablish the equilibrium of human reality. The final poem of *Trzy zimy*, entitled "Do księdza Ch." concludes with the significant sentence:

> Ziemia usta rozewrze, w jej dudniącej katedrze
> chrzest odbiorą ostatni poganie.
>
> ("Do księdza Ch.," *TZ*, 51)

> The earth will open wide its jaws and in its echoing cathedral
> The last pagans will be christened.
>
> ("To Father Ch.," tr. E.M.)

Consequently, the apocalypse will give unity back to the world, will return the banished people of contemporary civilization to God's Eden, and will bestow meaning on human existence which is suspended, it would seem, like a dry leaf amidst the gusts of the winds of history which are ruled by laws only they themselves know. That is how it seems to Anna from "Pieśń," who says:

> Ale nic nie ma we mnie prócz przestrachu,
> nic oprócz biegu ciemnych fal.
> Ja jestem wiatr, co niknąc w ciemnych wodach dmie,
> wiatrem jestem idącym a niewracającym się,
> pyłkiem dmuchawca na czarnych łąkach świata.
>
> ("Pieśń," *TZ*, 11)

> But there is nothing in me but fear,
> nothing but the running of dark waves.
> I am the wind that blows in dark waters, disappearing,
> I am the wind going out and not coming back,
> milkweed pollen on the black meadows of the world.
>
> ("Song," *SN*, 95)

Thus speaks, however, ignorance and the conviction that "besides my body I have nothing," the resigned faith that there is nothing beyond the time of human existence. Miłosz, however, unceasingly searches for the sort of order in which time would be not only human, but also divine, justifying the suffering, decline and fear of man. The fear of death and of the destruction of the world can only be overcome by the awareness that there is an element of some "higher" strategy for leading humanity back to the fullness of existence. Eschatological time, and therefore divine time, makes possible the existence of ordinary, human time, in which temporal existence is immersed. Therefore, paraphrasing Eliade, one could say Miłosz is experiencing the need to enter into this sacred and indestructible time, since a religious person,—it is difficult not to notice in *Trzy zimy* the presence of sacred motifs, numerous biblical-cryptic quotations, a tone of prayer and litany or a vision of Paradise—will unceasingly seek an opportunity to return to the world of "the beginning." However, a departure into the universe of eschatological myth may denote a breaking of ties with the present and a painful sense of alienation. Indeed, even R. Barthes assures us that "mythology is indubitably an acceptance of the world not as it is, but as it wishes to be."[19] It is difficult, however, to identify with a reality, to which assent is not expressed and in spite of which alternative models of the world are constructed on the basis of some higher order, which is given "without certainty," and whose hypothetical existence can only be supposed. The author of *Traktat o historii religii* (A Treatise on the History of Religion) answers:

> We have no basis according to which we can interpret the periodic return to the sacred time of the beginning as a rejection of the real world and an escape into dream as the world of the imagination. In direct opposition to this, here an ontological obsession is also making itself heard. . . . The desire for a reintegration of the time of the beginning is at once both the desire to discover the presence of gods and to attain a strong, fresh and pure world such as it was in *illo tempore*. That is at the same time a sacred hunger and a longing for being.[20]

It is also, at the same time, something more than Eliade says: a desire to reinterpret the image of the world, a dream of the kind of conception of history and of the truth of human biological duration which would be capable of justifying the catastrophic perspective and of consecrating the human condition. For it would be difficult to accept the kind of conception of existence of the Cosmos and Humanity which would make of them an existential Absurdity devoid of meaning and justification. Acceptance of such an image of the Universe would have to sanction the complete shattering of the code which is so unstable and in question at present. By entering into the sphere of eschatological myth, Miłosz's catastrophism provides value for human destiny and assures that it does not become a deterministic diagnosis depriving the individual and the collective of faith and hope. It permits one to trust that history is not a mechanism driven exclusively with the help of the evil inhering imminently in man, but that the threads of historical fulfillment are moved by the Demiurgic strategist who guides the world through the levels of the apocalypse towards brighter humanistic horizons.

Eschatological entanglement in time is, as it were, the first element determining human "being in the world." The second is man's spatial coordinates, i.e., his being situated at this and not another geographical point, his determination by specific social conditions, but not ignoring also natural or topographical factors. The poetic consciousness of a "street child" is one thing, while that of an artist formed in wild forests, bulrushes and swamps is another. P. Kuncewicz claims, that the philosophy of the second avant-garde, to which, after all, we relate Miłosz's poetry, "is stretched between the two opposing axes of nature and of history."[21] The qualification of this poetry through the world of nature is actually visible from practically the first poem written by this poet. Natural reality, with which the poet formed an alliance in *Poemat o czasie zastygłym* was a terrain of death and disintegration of a domain whose norm, like that of history, was the unconditional subordination of man to its own laws. The rules of the game into which the individual who exists in History enters, had been for him incomprehensible and absurd because of the contingency of the phenomena which question his right to life. The order of natural law, however, striking in its hieratic dignity and the inflexibility of its principles which pertain equally to man, seemed to the poet to be that kind of eternal order which one could not help but acknowledge.

Trzy zimy is like a continuation of that incessant dispute between man and the "earth" to which he is forever bound. "Pieśń" is a work in which this dispute is outlined in exceptionally stark relief. The choir sings a hymn in praise of the earth:

> Kręcą się kołowroty, ryby trzepocą się w sieciach,
> pachną pieczone chleby, toczą się jabłka po stołach,

wieczory schodzą po schodach, a schody z żywego ciała,
wsystko jest z ziemi poczęte, ona jest doskonała.
Chylą się ciężkie okręty, jadą miedziani bratowie,
kołyszą karkami zwierzęta, motyle spadają do mórz,
kosze wedruja o zmierzchu i zorza mieszka w jabłoni,
wszystko jest z ziemi poczęte, wszystko powróci do niej.

("Pieśń," *TZ*, 10)

The capstans are turning, fish shiver in the nets,
apples roll across tables, and the smell of baked bread rises,
down the steps goes the evening, and the steps are live flesh—
everything comes from the earth, she is perfect.
Heavy ships yaw, coppery brothers go sailing,
animals crane their necks, butterflies fall to the sea
and baskets wander at twilight. Dawn lives in an apple tree.
Everything comes from the earth and returns to her.

("Song," *SN*, 93)

The underlining of the naturalness of the rhythm to which the natural world is subjected, the emphasis on its eternal nature and on the primacy of the laws which it imposes on the entire biological universe, would seem to command an expectation of a tone of reconciliation and silent agreement on the part of man. And yet, Anna says:

Od ust ziemi chciwych odłącz mnie.
Od pieśni jej nieprawdziwych oczyść mnie.

("Pieśń," *TZ*, 10)

From earth's caresses, from her sweet greedy mouth, set me free.
Cleanse me of her untrue songs.

("Song," *SN*, 93)

This work is deeply ambivalent. On the one hand, man set against the silent enormity of nature calls out that there is in it "nothing but fear," while on the other hand, however, he knows that "every joy is from the earth, there is no gaiety without the earth." And there is no resolution to this human drama. Empty and sterile, with a painfully cracked ego, he dreams about an escape from the historical and natural order of laws, and yet he knows that it is only a hopeless struggle whose end will sooner or later be transformed into tragic resignation and subordination to "the earth."

It is difficult not to notice, however, that not only nature is active: it is not only nature which incessantly forces her way into man's consciousness, making him humbly bow his head before her order of laws. Likewise, man incessantly intervenes in this world, subjecting it to his destructive activity.

kłębi się przemieniony ogień czworga nieb,
i tli się złotą trawą ziemia kędy szedł
cień, ślady nóg w popękanym wyciskając żwirze.
. . . .
Mży śnieg. I drzewo każde, przełamane, krwawi.
("Ptaki," *TZ*, 8)

a transformed fire of four heavens swirls
and the ground flames up with golden grass
where he, a shadow, passed, imprinting his trace on cracked gravel.
. . . .
A snow flurry. And every tree, broken, bleeds.
("Birds," tr. E.M.)

It is "the earth" which becomes the bearer of the stigma of annihilation, and it is her images which become monstrous under the eye of the prophet who senses catastrophe all around. It is, after all, from her that Miłosz develops the majority of his catastrophic images. The apparently indifferent landscape is transformed in his poem into a land of mysterious, dark signs. It becomes branded by human fear and suffering, and the now animated elements become participants in the cosmic drama.

Z pod ziemi rosło światło, zimny blask przeświecał
przez sierść czujnie leżących zwierząt pręgowaną,
przez piwnice budowli zbryzganych dnia pianą,
i widać było skrzydła drzew lecąca w dymie.
("Bramy arsenału," *TZ*, 12)

Light grew up from under the ground, a cold glow shone through
The stripped fur of the animals in their alert repose,

through the cellars of buildings sprinkled with the foam of day.
And the wings of trees were flying in the haze.
("The Gates of Arsenal," tr. E.M.)

The cold radiance of annihilation permeates the entire natural universe which is included as the current actor in the cast of the apocalyptic performance. It seems that it is even possible to speak of the correspondence of the "events" of the human world with the world of nature.

Wyżej szła chmura, a nad nią spienione
stada gwiazd gnały i parły motory
trójśmigłych statków. Złoty krzyż wieziono,
jedwabny sztandar i hełmy z żelaza.

Wiatr był na ziemi. Dzwoniły jabłonie
owocem żółtym, i jarzębiny chrzęst.
("Wieczorem wiatr," *TZ*, 31)

High up a cloud moved and above it
herds of stars galloped. The engines
of three-propellered planes dashed, carrying a golden cross,
a silk banner and helmets of iron.

Wind swept the earth. The apple-trees rang
with their yellow fruit and the rowan trees rattled.
("Wind in the Evening," tr. E.M.)

Just as in *Pan Tadeusz* natural elements seem to be allied with man, seething angrily during the course of battle, so in *Trzy zimy* each appearance of martial accents is tied to changes in the natural background. The rhythmic character of blossoming and harvest corresponds to the time of creation and work, while the wobbling of stars and poplars and the flashing of bloody crosses and glows in the sky corresponds to the time of destruction. This "alliance," however, is imposed on her by force. Man, with his destructive power, upsets her order and calm leading to a parallelism of destructive rhythm. Essentially, however, nature—despite the inflexibility of her decalogue—does not cease to be a constantly open proposition for man, one which offers him specific advantages to be gained from the recognition of his dependance relative to her.

pierwszy blask dnia, co stąpa wzdłuż strumieni
z wysokich gór nad mgłę różowych jezior
i grzeje oczy tych, co przystanęli, z dłonią u czoła.
zakończywszy noc.
("Dytyramb")

The first gleam of day strolls along the streams
down the high mountains over the mist of rosy lakes,
and warms the eyes of those who stand shading their brows
after having finished their night.
("Dithyramb," tr. E.M.)

She is provident and even, we might say, in her own way, coquettish.

Czuła ciemność pochyla się nad czołem,
jak ukochana nad ciałem śpiącego
i wąska smużka zawartej w niej światłości
przemywa powieki. Idźmy—mówi—Idźmy.
("Dytyramb")

A tender darkness leans over the head
like a beloved over the body of a lover
and the narrow streak of light it contains
washes the eyelids. Let's go, it says, let's go.
("Dithyramb," tr. E.M.)

Kuncewicz is right then, when he writes that

> here nature is drawn in its charms and grandeur, it promises calm and quiet. "Happiness" and "purposefulness" are most often expressed by a representation of the process of growth. Leaves grow, grass sways, trees blossom and bear fruit. There is joy in these images, never noisy, never violent, never justifiable. It is joy in the very fact of existence, in the very fact of growth, and also joy which does not need motivation, like the joy of parents in having a child.[22]

At the base of this natural protection, Gea herself, mother and protectress, seems to inhere, desiring to spread her affectionate love over man lost in the midst of events, struggling in the inability to discover his own place. Her purposeful activity—blossoming, growth, ripening, internal harmony and calm, beauty and harmony—are joined in one rhythm which seems to bewitch by its organization and precision. It is possible to find in it everything which is lacking in the human extra-natural environment. However, joining himself with that order demands of man a sacrifice—the recognition of himself as a particle of that harmonious element, the equation of his destiny with that of a bird, a tree, a leaf or a stone. The recognition of oneself—a tiny particle of the cosmos is able to guarantee man a return to the lost order. In "Hymn" we read:

> . . . Ja, wierny syn czarnoziemu, powrócę do czarnoziemu
> jakby życia nie było,
> jakby pieśni, i słowa tworzyło
> nie moje serce, nie moja krew,
> nie moje trwanie,
> ale sam głos niewiadomy, bezosobowy,
> sam łopot fal, sam wiatrów chór, samo wysokich drzew
> jesienne kołysanie.
>
> ("Hymn," *TZ*, 15)

> . . . I, faithful son of black earth, will return to the black earth.
> as if my life had not been,
> as if not by my heart, not my blood
> not my duration
> had created words and songs
> but an unknown, impersonal voice,
> only the flapping of waves, only the choir of winds,
> and the autumnal sway
> of the tall trees.
>
> ("Hymn," *CP*, 13)

The image of the cosmos as a musical sphere has its origins as far back as Pythagoras, who suffered from the fact that between the chaos of human affairs and the harmony of the cosmos there is no understanding at all, and that only subordination of man to the ideal rhythm of the "heavens" and to nature which copies their order will allow the construction of an alliance between these two different worlds. Miłosz seems to share that opinion: joining oneself with the natural order means the possibility of discovering an internal order and a harmonious participation in the eternal order of things. That is still one more road which crosses into the infernal consciousness of one's own epoch and which leads to a "holy" space, which still remains in the power of Providence. "For a religious man the rhythms of vegetation reveal . . . the mystery of life and of the act of creation, and also of renewal, of youth and of immortality," writes Eliade.[23] The attempt to take part in this mystery is a chance for a return to the Garden, remnants of which have survived in the world of nature, which alone has not changed the principles of its duration, and in whose laws the imprint of the work of creation is reflected.

> Dojrzałem, moje ciało jest czułą kołyską
> dla mocy, w których płaczu zawiera się wszystko,
> leżą w pięknym posłaniu i miłość i głód.
> Wiatr swobodnych poranków we włosach powiewa
> i jabłko, ciężkie jabłko, sen rajskiego drzewa
> tuczy sie, potrącane końcem lekkich stóp.
>
> ("Do księdza Ch.," *TZ*, 51)

> I have matured, my body is a tender cradle
> for powers whose lament tells everything,
> it makes a fine bed both for hunger and love.
> The wind of clear mornings flutters in my hair
> and the apple, heavy apple, the dream of the paradise tree
> rolls, touched by the points of nimble feet.
>
> ("To Father Ch.," tr. E.M.)

A return to the world of perpetual rhythm is equally, however, a return to awareness of the inevitability of death and disintegration, to the chilling conviction that a new alliance between the living may be totally achieved only in the next world. The great reconciliation of opposites is achieved "on the other side," in the Kingdom of Charon:

> nadpływa sternik, zarzuca sznur jedwabny
> i przywiązuje jedno do drugiego,
> i sypie na przyjaciół, wrogów dawnych,
> garsteczkę śniegu.
>
> ("Posąg małżonków," *TZ*, 39)

> A helmsman comes, throws a silken rope
> and binds us tightly to each other,
> then he pours on friends, once enemies,
> a handful of snow.
>
> ("The Statue of a Couple," *SP*, 58)

Czesław Miłosz does not leave his contemporary a great deal of hope. On the one hand, he tells him to believe that by accepting the providential vision of history he will free himself from doubt in the meaning of the world, that existing in history he exists also in "sacred" time. On the other hand, however, he persuades him that, by accepting that rhythm of the world to which nature is subordinated, he bestows upon his existence a divine sanction, that in discovering a tie with the biological world he returns to Eden. This resigned awareness is the only consolation which the poet is able to propose. Arcadian poetry, which is manifested in the legend of the Isles of Bliss, The Golden Age or The Gardens, and which promises an escape from the problems of civilization, from the insufficiencies of existence or finally from nonhuman complications, also restrains itself from a totally idyllic image. The residents of Arcadia, although they are freed from many cares which demand from them a certain foresight, are not, however, ultimately liberated from human fear and imperfections. It frequently befell them to suffer from unrequited love or the fear of death. Miłosz also does not promise such freedom in his poetry. He does not even attempt to enhance the image of nature. Certainly, she ensures certain advantages, extends her care, provides all manner of good, thrusts the individual into a certain order which is in harmony with daily and annual cycles, but her poisonous, realistic contour does not suffer destruction. The myth of the Garden is based on a realistic skeleton. Co-participation in sacred time in no way means liberation from presence in the historical cataclysm. At the most it would explain the meaning of this sacrifice. Stepping into a space whose rules are made credible by an act of creation, also does not imply any specific privileges, but only guarantees the thrill of rubbing against a higher order which is reflected in the code of nature. Here the principles of the coexistence of forms of being are clearly specified "right from the outset." This order is given from above, and there is no room for any fluctuation of values whatsoever. Perhaps, then, striving for the eternal order of being, perhaps the study of the moral alphabet, must be begun anew, perhaps in the contemporary world that is the sole source of order on which a human being can base itself.

I tak to jest, że wtedy, gdy nas łączy
ze światem miłość smutkiem doświadczona
nagle otwiera się tama milczenia,
szum, wrzenie skrzydeł, pieśń barw w nas przemawia,
wróżyć umiemy z nieba, z drzew i nagle
widać, jak to ma być opowiedziane, co naszych ust na swoją
spowiedź chce.
Słów trzeba użyć czystych, niech najlżejszy nawet ślad
wspommień o dniach i nocach przeżytych ich nie plami.
Bo po to są tygodnie, miesiące i lata, po to ból mądrości,
aby nauczyć się mówić na drzewo: drzewo, na człowieka:
człowiek, i na gwiazdę: gwiazda,
aby z oparów lęku wyprowadzić ziemię
nową, jak Boga kształt, który ją wskrzesza.

("Dytyramb")

And so it is, that when we are joined
to the world in love touched by sadness
suddenly the gate of silence is open,
sound ebullience of wings, song speaks in us,
we can tell fortunes from the sky, from the trees and all at once
one can see, how that which needs our lips for its confession,
ought to be said.
One must use pure words, even the slightest shade
of recollections about experienced days and nights should not taint
them.
Weeks, months and years exist, the pain of wisdom exists for the
same reason—
that we can learn to call a tree: a tree, to call a man:
a man, and to call a star: a star,
to lead from the mists of fear a new earth
like God's shape who raises it from the dead.

("Dithyramb," tr. E.M.)

A total union with the world, an appeal to the first letters of human experience and the discovery of one's own point in the cosmos form a basis from which it is possible to base the poet's third journey—after the journeys through the time of the Apocalypse and through the Garden of nature—this time into the act of Creation.

The cautions of Cassandra, the glossolalia of the entranced Pythia, the prophecies of Sybill, the visions of Elijah and the revelations of John of Patmos are only in certain parts understandable to the general public. The direct "content" of a prophetic revelation is securely hidden under a multilayered growth of mysterious signs, images and chaotic and disorganized visions. The real meaning of a prophecy is closed within a thicket of morbid imaginings and shreds of terrifying dreams, amid restless hallucinations and illusions, submerged in a mobile magma of symbols, unintelligible gestures and presentiments, carried on a wave of seemingly uncontrolled inspiration which extends beyond its own time and space. The intellectual structure of a prophecy is generally simple and uncomplicated but the disengagement of it from this symbolic flow of words is not possible. The prophet, having the gift of the charisma of seeing future events is only a faulty transmitter of truths which by the will of the gods trickle through his mouth. It is not unambiguous and easily verbalized human truths which he transmits to the world. His mission is the fullest possible articulation of the flood of impressions, thoughts, and images which have been sent by the grace of God. The visionary is a member of the collective but is at the same time situated, as it were, beyond it. His fate is alienation and inspired madness which transfers his soul to other spheres of being.

One of the oldest attributes of poeticity is precisely inspiration, prophetic ecstasy, a visionary madness. Already Plato in the *Phaedrus* gave, as the first and fundamental kind of insanity, prophetic, i.e., Appollinian, madness, and confused it later in the *Ion* with poetic madness. It was for him beyond doubt that this state is a "beautiful illness," a radiation of divine benevolence, a summoning to participate in the ideal world. The inconceivability and incomprehensibility of the divine universe functions such that an artistic "report" of the journey to the limitlessness of absolute knowledge, from the outset, must be tainted by the stamp of impossibility. That which does not fit into any human categories cannot be told. It must become a pitiful approximation in language and images, a reduction of those which is inexpressible in the sphere of verbal communications. The artist who has experienced a vision is in a tragic situation. He is under an obligation to transmit the mysteries to which he has been initiated, but he knows in advance that such a task is totally inachievable, that his every effort is tainted with the stamp of falsity. He chooses, therefore, the lesser and, giving up the idea of communication, accepts being incomprehensible, and speaks with the pure voice of prophetic madness, without reflecting on the possible "usefulness" of his glossolalia. If he tends in a Promethean gesture, to bestow artistic meaning on his mysterious voice which falters on his incompetent, human lips, he will deform the "true" form of the message entrusted to him. If, however, he trusts that there is no other way and that "trzeba" ["it is necessary"] as Miłosz says in "Dytyramb," not to worry about "jak to ma być opowiedziane, co naszych ust na swoją spowiedź chce," ["how that which needs our lips for its confession, ought to be said" (tr. E.M.)], then perhaps some particle of the revealed truth will flow before the eyes of humanity, which are sunk in the darkness of ignorance.

No small amount of pride is necessary to recognize oneself as a chosen and summoned person, to recognize that precisely through our mouths, through our dream-catastrophic visions and through our panopticon of imagination the Divine Deimonian speaks. Already in the "Powolna rzeka," Miłosz expressed his conviction concerning the unusual nature of his own poetic mission. In *Trzy zimy*, we can find a great deal of evidence bearing witness to the sense of his own strength and the extraordinary nature of his own role:

a mnie jest dana siła.
("Hymn," *TZ*, 15)

and to me strength is given.
("Hymn," *CP*, 13)

Nie mam ani mądrości, ani umiejętności, ani wiary,
ale dostałem siłę, ona rozdziera świat.
("Hymn," *TZ*, 16)

I have no wisdom, no skills, and no faith
but I received strength, it tears the world apart.
("Hymn," *CP*, 13–14)

Więc może za mną też oczami pływa
ten, co zrozumie pracę moich rąk
("O młodszym bracie," *TZ*, 20)

And so, somebody else perhaps waits for me
able to comprehend the work of my hands.
("About My Younger Brother," tr. E.M.)

Potrzykroć winno się obrócić koło
ludzkich zaślepień, zanim ja bez lęku
spojrzę na władzę śpiącą w mojem ręku,
("Powolna rzeka," *TZ*, 37)

Three times must the wheel of blindness
turn, before I look without fear at the power
sleeping in my own hand,
("Slow River," *CP*, 20)

Ale wędrując ciemną chmurą moich źrenic
widziałeś może gwiazdę, obok ptaka śpiącą,
gwiazdę łagodnych toni, podwodnych ramienic,
niech będzie twoim światłem, . . .
("Awanturnik,"* *TZ*, 47)

Yet while you wandered in my eyes' dark cloud
you saw perhaps a star asleep there by a bird,
a star of gentle depths, of sea vegetations,
let it be your light, . . .
("The Adventurer," tr. E.M.)

i odsłaniałem dziwy z głębi moich oczu,
wiedząc, że tam odnaleźć można krwawy wieniec,
("Awanturnik," *TZ*, 46)

And I uncovered wonders hidden in my eyes,
knowing that one can find there a wreath of blood,
("The Adventurer," tr. E.M.)

The poet asserts, to be sure, that his own prophetic predispositions fill him with fear, that first the scales of blindness must fall from man's eyes. Yet it is he, the inspired artist, touched with the stigma of an insane calling, able to penetrate the verdicts of history, who is summoned to the mission of revelation. The Appollinian madness of clairvoyance becomes the lot of the poet of the interwar period.

Mówią mu: "Ty masz wielką gorączkę, ten płynny
żar źrenice ci objął od niedawna chyba,

*This poem is a translation of P. de la Tour du Pin, "D'Un Avanturier," in *Une Somme de Poésie*.

to jest dziwna choroba, co u dzieci bywa,
w twoich oczach zmienionych prześwieca świat inny,
niż w jego, niż w ich . . ."
("Awanturnik," *TZ*, 45)

They tell him: you have a high fever,
this inflammation of pupils gripped you recently,
it is a strange illness that happens to children,
a different world transpires through your altered vision,
different from the one found in his eyes or theirs . . .
("The Adventurer," tr. E.M.)

The madness of the contemporary Cassandra of the Żagary Group is particularly sophisticated. To prognosticate in ecstatic exultation the approach of an era of murder and the disintegration of values and to pseudonymize its real contours through a whirling network of shocking visions and images is the privilege of individuals of highly artistic sensitivity. However, to recognize at the same time that this creative effort aspires to the role of the revealed word is to step onto the path along which, up to now, only the romantic heralds and biblical prophets have trodden. What, then, is a poetry which strives to reveal a demiurgic conception of history and to indicate the points at which the presence of the Creator is reflected, but which, at the same time, with inflexible certainty and dignity erects a theatre of the Day of Judgement and the Day of Salvation? *Trzy zimy* is a kind of repetition of the Biblical Revelation, a new and contemporary version of the Apocalypse according to Czesław Miłosz.

As to how he decided on this form, the poet speaks very enigmatically. During the 1930s, the author of "Siena" wrote that poetry "is fed by ignorance, darkness, fairy tales and mystery."[24] Critics have aptly grasped these features of his second collection.

> The most outstanding feature of Miłosz's poetry from this period is the need for fairy tales, to play with concreteness in an unreal and alogical world, and for ways to use metaphors in imitation of the structure of dream. Above this world hovers the ultramarine threat of catastrophe and senselessness expressed with an expressionistic pathos.[25]
>
> Fantastic visions which are plastic and filled with poetic expression, numerous symbolic-imagenial elements with a complex and often unclear

> symbolism, self-contained poetic images joined only by a homogeneous emotional-reflectional stream—all of this becomes a meditation on the passing of things and a presentiment of the approaching years of danger and disaster. He makes reality unreal, and he creates a world reminiscent of a dream-world and ruled by laws of free and irrational associations which express a continually returning presentiment.[26]

> His poetic images—detached from reality, entering into a land of pure fiction, absolutely untranslatable into a language of practical life—have a thoroughly static character. Their immaterial expressivity in this fixed and solemn static quality seems to be classical.[27]

> Miłosz . . . is an inspired lyrical poet, if not to say possessed, and his oeuvre reminds one of exorcisms which he performs on himself. He carries out symbolic judgement on his own ego . . .[28]

One of the fundamental characteristics of prophetic literature and of the books of the Apocalypse is the esoteric quality of its language. The enigmatic content and mysterious form of these works function so that the reader who is put in their presence must guess the meaning more so than he is, in fact, able to grasp it conceptually. Apocalyptics demands hermeneutics. No interpretation, however, nor any manner of explanation of it, is able to approach the essence of the thing, because, by its own formation and nature it is unknowable. Alogical, complicated system of metaphors, expressionism, dreaminess, fantastic, unreality and an atmosphere of danger—these are the most frequently appearing terms related to the imaginary world traced by Miłosz in *Trzy zimy* and in his slightly later works of the 1930s. They all, without exception, aptly characterize the image of this lyrical poetry and enlighten us as to which artistic means aided in the construction of the contemporary apocalypse. Their artistic combination, i.e., the making of a complicated network of interdependences through which they can appeal to the reader with unusual power and suggestiveness, made the critics treat this part of Miłosz's achievement as a self-contained entity detached from experiential reality, as a projection of an unbridled and totally uncontrolled catastrophically oriented poetic imagination. Any attempts whatsoever to create an analytic and semantic unity of meaning from these pronouncements from the outset seemed senseless. Mention was made of the atmosphere of the danger and uncertainty of tomorrow, of the stigma of annihilation suspended above the world and about the images of the cosmic disintegration of the universe. The esoteric quality of the catastrophic language seemed to be only a tool used in the uttering of prognosticating revelations and in poetic aesthetic experiments. Catastrophic danger and literary autotelism appear to be the two main leitmotifs of the literary critics' statements which attempt to untangle the riddles of this collection. Moreover, these efforts must have appeared to be somewhat illusory in the face of the *expressis verbis* articulated convictions that this work should be treated as a self-contained whole, not susceptible to interpretational segmentation and revealing its value only as a "complete" vision. Therefore, the fundamental value of *Trzy zimy* was discerned, above all, in its emotional aura, in the atmosphere of apocalyptic gravity and in the charm of its imagerial-visionary construction.

At the same time, however, in practically every statement dedicated to this collection, the terms "symbolism" or "symbolic quality" appear. This is not accidental. Just as apocalyptic esoterism contains heavy accretions of eschatological symbolism, so twentieth century understanding of symbol has very often identified it with autonomism, with a recognition of it as a self-contained entity. When writing, therefore, about the symbolic quality of Czesław Miłosz's catastrophic world, his esthetic autotelism is stressed first of all, and then, in some sense, it is recognized as the quintessence of refined poeticity. What is more, this corresponds exceptionally well with the reflection of M. Podraza-Kwiatkowska, who states that "the conception . . . of a symbol as a creation endowed with its own autonomous existence is, in fact, nothing other than the identification of it with poetry in general."[29] This is so, essentially because the symbolic world is a space in which the point of creation of a new reality is reached, of such a transmutation of real and imagined elements that they compose into totally new qualities, different and radiating with still unknown lights. Such, also, in fact, is the poetic Universe constructed by the author of *Ocalenie* (Rescue) in his second collection from the interwar period. Alienated from the real world, seductive in its mysterious and unusual variability, pulsating with unclear meanings which provoke the reader to a series of divergent associations, it seems to be an autonomous aesthetic quality. But is this all? We have already indicated the presence in this collection of two eschatological "messages" which follow a twisting and capricious line through the unclear images and visions. Still, how does this problem look when observed through the prism of the symbol, classically understood?

Eschatological doctrine is the chief trait of apocalyptism. Czesław Miłosz's poetry of the interwar period is not free from it. The mysterious, sublime, symbolic and enigmatic esoteric quality of prophecy, which repels attempts to conceptually and intellectually master it, is very highly visible in the hermetic world of the poetically autonomous catastrophic visions of *Trzy zimy*. At the same time, however, the same intellectual model keeps shining through:

> With the prediction of future liberation is the result of the intervention of the Son of God and The Messiah, of the return from slavery and of the reunification of generations, of praise for the New Jerusalem, of an era of material well-being, peace and happiness, is tied the foretelling of the defeat of the enemy and their subordination to the God of Israel, of the Judgement of peoples by God, and finally of the cosmic catastrophes which will accompany the final revelation of God and the resurrection of bodies, bringing annihilation to the evil and happiness to the righteous.[30]

Hidden beneath the symbolic logogryph of images, dreams, visions and signs, there is the outline of a different, higher reality, into which, through the thicket of prophetic revelations, the human individual, plunged in the darkness of ignorance and doubts, desires to penetrate.

What is symbol? The answer is difficult and not unequivocal. M. Podraza-Kwiatkowska, the author of *Symbol i symbolika w poezji Młodej Polski* (Symbol and Symbolism in the Poetry of "Young Poland"), developing a series of ever broader formulations, arrives at the following definition:

> A symbol is an equivalent—individual, unconventional, deprived of pedagogical and ornamental functions, ambiguous and imprecise, and based on the allusions of specific emotions—of such qualities which, because they are not clearly crystallized qualities, do not have adequate designations in the language system. Such a symbol, expanded into a series of images and analogies, occasionally into an entire work, and as a result of a total merging of the levels of sign and meaning, can become an autonomous existent which cannot be translated into discursive language.[31]

These expanding definitional amplifications make the fundamental assumption, however, that a symbol is an equivalent of those qualities which cannot be verbalized, that it only suggests, and does not express them. After all it is not accidental that it has such close ties with idealistic philosophy which posited beyond the "real" yet illusory and apparent human world the existence of permanent, stable and indestructible spheres of existence. Precisely this "real" world is actually only a symbol of real being, which is the proper point of reference for man's cognitive efforts. Human art cannot therefore be anything other than—one would like to repeat after Morice—the revealer of Infinity. Thus, the symbol, above all can become the fundamental tool for attaining to this mysterious sphere. In the first number of *Zdrój* we read a characteristic declaration: "Symbols serve man in the expression of the Inexpressible, in the intellectualization of the mysteries of the Unknown, which momentarily dazzle man's mind in brief flashes."[32] Przesmycki formulated it in the same unambiguous manner:

> Beauty without the background of the infinite . . . cannot provide satisfaction. He is an artist, poet, creator and genius whose imagination encompasses both sides of the world, who in every manifestation of the external world, in every stirring of thought or feeling, is able to symbolically emphasize the element of infinity beside the sensory element.[33]

What is characteristic here is that the idealistic conception of the existence of essential being, of a sphere of objective and permanent although hidden qualities, was usually tied to the phenomena of *anamnesis*, about which Plato had already said that it is a repetition of that which at some other time had been granted the human soul to see. This institutional epistemology of the symbolists, deriving precisely from the Platonic-Plotinian tradition, permitted the artist, by way of internal illumination to attain to the essence of being. At the same time, according to M. Podraza-Kwiatkowska, this drive to the unknown, which with such resistance reveals the outlines of its "pre-existence," is tightly linked with one of the principles of poetic creativity: "the principle of creation in a spontaneous manner, in sudden moments of revelation."[34]

Symbolic representation, therefore, as one of the key features of Miłosz's oeuvre from the period of *Trzy zimy*, performs, as it were, two key functions: it creates an autonomous hermetic world of the imagination which strives towards a region of pure poeticity not corrected by anything except internal artistic necessity. The second function, which operates simultaneously, and in which once again the antynomic character of this poetry is manifested, refers us to the domain of pure essential being, to a world of absolute incarnations, which cannot be "explained" in an unambiguous and complete manner. "God, the absolute, spirit, immortality, eternity and infinity," says Matuszewski, "are bottomless abysses. . . .

One must express oneself concerning the great mysteries of existence in a mysterious manner."[35] And such is also Miłosz's prophesying: mysterious, threatening, visionary, pathetic, dignified, unclear, radiating with the somewhat alarming charm of the "Final Word." The creator of the apocalypse, convinced of the importance of his revelatory mission, speaks with the full gravity and pathos due a historical moment. With enormous certainty and power he appeals to his visions and inspirations which have their source in the voice of God. "These visions and voices," we read in the *Podręczna encyklopedia biblijna* (Biblical Reference Encyclopedia),

> were formed mainly from either internal or imaginational or again intellectual impressions. They always, however, produced the profound conviction in the prophets, that God Himself had spoken to them, and therefore when they passed them on to the people, they asserted with total conviction, testifying to subjective truth, that it was really the Word of God.[36]

It is, however, unlikely that a twentieth-century artist, even if deeply convinced that he has been granted a vision of future apocalyptic events which according to him will inscribe themselves on the eschatological pattern of history, would be able to so fanatically consider himself as the "mouthpiece of God." Ultimately, *Trzy zimy* is just literature, a small volume of poetry by a still young writer who stylized it as a contemporary Book of the Apocalypse. In its "deep" structure it, of course, conceals a Christian credo, nevertheless in the first order of things, it is a literary transformation of the prophetic book expressed with the aid of the conceptual-imagerial storehouse of avant-garde forms, referring to the traditional categories of apocalyptic formulations. Miłosz sometimes speaks like an inspired prophet, attributing to himself a "power" which is not given to others, but at the same time as an artist who doubts and who persuades us unceasingly of the uncertainty and instability of everything; he cannot, after all, choose to speak with the voice of a prophet. His truths are very often concealed behind a screen of intermediary forms. They are proclaimed by the lyrical interlocutors of these poems (like Anna and the choir in "Pieśń" or the Guide and the Pupil in "Dialog"); they are attributed to an adversary or "listener" who is not precisely identified ("Do księdza Ch.," "Powolna rzeka," "Roki," "Ptaki," "Hymn"); they are written into a lyrical, objectified narrative ("Bramy arsenału"); they are declared through a collective subject ("O książce," "Wieczorem wiatr," "Posąg małżonków"); they assume the character of a "tale" or a parable or a fairy tale ("O młodszym bracie," "Kołysanka"); or they are suspended in the teachings imparted to the Pupil by the Master ("Dialog," "Do księdza Ch.," "O młodszym bracie"). Yet none of above-mentioned forms exists in its pure state. They build up upon each other, completing, sometimes excluding, producing an astounding and mobile structure of polyphonic pronouncements, of a multivoiced choir, which obsessively repeats over and over the same truths, but it is impossible to abstract a personal subject. It is, of course, Miłosz himself. Nevertheless such careful veiling of his own voice amidst the prophesying agony of those who see the future is here significant. Perhaps the right to full and individual *inspiratio prophetica* has been taken away from the twentieth-century prophet, but it is maintained by an artist who ascribes his eschatological convictions to his lyrical heroes and stylizes his poetic collection on the *Book of Revelations*.

A. Fiut wrote that

> Mickiewicz could have considered himself a prophet and herald of the Kingdom of God because at that time something like an expansion of the sphere of the sacred occurred. "The Books of the Polish Nation" became in this situation the new "Bible," a Holy Book, the poet became the revealer of divine verdicts and Lithuania . . . a model of Paradise, a world-garden. All this, of course, is now inaccessible to the contemporary poet.[37]

Is it, however, really so? Indeed, it is certainly not accidental that the author of "Dowód nietożsamości" ("Non-I.D. Card") had previously carried out reflections on the essence of the poetic myth present in Miłosz's lyrical poetry. He proved that we have here to do with an incomplete and degraded myth, a myth which has not yet ceased to be itself but is not yet able to be a complete myth. It would seem to retain its religious functions, but at the same time it is not able in a complete manner to give meaning to reality. That is to say, desiring to satisfy his longing for absolute values and struggling with the pressure of alienation, he reached out for the language of primeval imaginations, but he did so with the awareness of the incompleteness of his efforts. Only a complete lack of trust in his prophetic mission and resignation from inscription in a mythical paradigm seem to testify to his total doubt in the meaning of his revelatory vocation. But yet Miłosz, in showing the collapse of the contemporary world, declaring the instability of norms and codes of values, divesting the individual of faith and the opportunity of evading the verdict of catastrophe, and presenting reality as a sphere of action of absurd laws and historical phenomena does not totally deprive man of hope. He also does not promise him anything extraordinary. Quite the opposite: he asserts that the only axioms of reality are death, destruction of the material foundations of reality, a sense of the meaninglessness of existence, an eternally unsatisfied hunger for metaphysical values and the inevitable erosion of all interpersonal ties. However, he adds at the same time: one can be tempted to reconstruct an absolutist model of the world, one can postulate the kind of vision of the world which will not be an acknowledgement of the Satanism of the Absurd, one can search on earth for divine fulfillments which justify human suffering and death. And, finally, one can return from the modern, resigned, anthropological image to the idealist tradition, as the only tradition which does not condemn man to Chaos. And it is precisely such an effort, such a purpose which is at the base of *Trzy zimy*. Miłosz hypostasizes, he does not say that THIS is for certain, only he asserts that *the acceptance of such assumptions also implies a saving order, one which can integrate humanity in the search for the light of Truth.* Only a cognitive effort and the acceptance of the proposed model of the world which ensconces existence in essence bestows meaning on humanity.

> . . . w węzeł gordyjski jesteśmy spleceni
> z krzywdą, a z pleców spływa nam królewski płaszcz,
> podbity krzywdą złorzeczeń, skargą uciśnionych.
> I nie rozetnie splotu obnażony miecz,
> i nie zagłuszą krzywd armatnie koła,
> ale pomoże mowa tak rozumna, że sama w prądzie natchnienia się
> chyli
> jak zieleń na dnie błyskawicznych rzek,
> że przygotowuje tylko bujne łoże
> i czeka, aż ją dotknie duch i zamilknie spór
> o to, jak to ma być opowiedziane, co naszych ust na swoją spowiedź
> chce.
>
> ("Dytyramb")

> We are tangled in a Gordian knot
> with evil, but from our shoulders flows a royal coat
> lined with curses and the grievance of the oppressed.

And the bare blade cannot cleave this tangle,
and wheeling cannons cannot silence wrongs,
but speech will help, a speech so clever
that in the current of inspiration it will bow
like verdure on the bottom of swift rivers
which prepares a rich bed
and waits until it is touched by spirit
and the dispute how should be said that
which needs our lips for confession, will be silenced.
("Dithyramb," tr. E.M.)

Since only a creativity which illumines the meaning of the paradoxes of the world is able to provide satisfaction, it is therefore necessary to restore its revelatory quality which, over the course of centuries, has been lost. It must again become the Holy Book, The Book of Knowledge of the Universe, The Revealed Logos. For Heraclitis, logos means the law-like regularity of the world, for the stoics it was *ananka* or cosmic reason, the neo-Platonists discerned in it a hypostasis of divine reason, and in Christian theology the Word symbolizes the Son of God. In each case we have to do with a search for the kind of thinking and the kind of "language" which would reflect the Order of the World. The prophecy of Czesław Miłosz is like an effort to inscribe oneself into a third myth—the myth of the Holy Word, into poetry as a replica of the Logic of the World, into a versified Book of Wisdom.

The apocalyptic prophet of 1936 A.D. must then feel that he has been called. In the litanical "Brama wieczoru" we read:

Z naszego plemienia był ten, którego dotknęłaś wielkim bólem
i kazałaś mu zejść do piekieł z przewodnikiem leśnej głuszy.
Któremu ukazywałaś po tym niebieskie zbocze raju,
Kiedy na ziemi jutrzenka wody rumieniła.
("Brama wieczoru")

From our race was the one whom you touched with a great affliction
and told him to descend to Hell with the wilderness guide.
Afterwards you showed him the blue slopes of Paradise
while on earth the dawn reddened the waters.
("The Gate of Evening," tr. E.M.)

He is the one who, amidst the signs of inevitable annihilation painted time and again on the pages of the poetry of the interwar period, discerned the necessity of appealing to some higher level "so that we would cherish / so that we would feel on our faces the caress of the warmth of your [of the Mother of God]* palm, the calling of invisible truths." The Apocalypse as the trial of ultimate things restores Man to Truth and Truth to Poetry.

> . . . czyż to jest pycha, kiedy wiara nam się odsłania
> i łaska nie widzenia, ale dotykania
> do prawd i dziejów, które w ludziach śpią?
> Grzeszny, nędzny i nagi jestem przed tym który włada
> i w czarny piach, w surowe wody rzuca mną.
> Módl się Jerzy. Dziękuj, że ci przeczuwać dano
> to, co nadejdzie, jak noc nadchodzi po dniu.
> . . . .
> A to nie będzie zdarzenie, jakiego się boją kobiety, aby im towarzyszy
> nocy nie zabrano,
> ani nieszczęście narodów, którego lękać się trzeba.
> Ale wielkie tajemnic wyjaśnienie,
> czerwona puszcza rozdarta przez sine płomienie
> ażeby spełnił się ogień, dotychczas niewytłumaczony.
>
> ("List 1/X 1935 r.")[38]

> . . . is it pride to maintain that faith reveals itself
> together with the grace, not of seeing, but of touching
> truths of the past that lie asleep in people?
> I am sinful, miserable and naked before Him who reigns
> and throws me into black sand, rough waters.
> Pray, George, give thanks for your premonition
> of things that must arrive, as night follows day.
> . . . .
> And that will not be just an event feared by women
> as it takes the companions of their nights away,
> nor a misfortune of nations, which nations should dread,
> but a great unravelling of mysteries,
> a red wilderness torn apart by blue flames,
> so that fire, until now unexplained, be fulfilled.
>
> ("Letter," tr. E.M.)

* Author's note

Czesław Miłosz's book of the apocalypse is closing. What was to be revealed has been revealed, what was to be negated has been negated. Poetry on the threshold of the day of the end of the world gives up its ludificative privileges, and asks about that which is most difficult and most important. It also tries to give an answer to the question of what one should believe in when "the seventh angel blows its trumpet, and rain mixed with blood falls on the earth": in the fact that the earth is not given as prey to nothingness, that human history is not in the power of the Urizen of meaninglessness, that every phenomenon, every situation and every existence is *justified,* since in "every man you see the sign of the living God." The darkness of the apocalypse is falling, and it seems there is not hope, still:

> spojrzenie odnajduje spojrzenie dawno przepadłe,
> powieki otwierają się nad niebieską źrenicą zaginionych.
> To są gody wielkiego spotkania, silniejszego niż śmierć i oschłość.
> ("Brama poranku")

> a glance meets a glance that has disappeared long ago,
> eyelids open showing the blue eyes of the missing.
> This is a feast of great reunion, stronger than death and coldness of
> heart.
> ("The Gate of Dawn," tr. E.M.)

Miłosz's poetic thought incessantly seems to outstrip his publicist-essayist statements in the interwar years. Just as *Poemat o czasie zastygłym* was to illustrate the social passions of the poet but became a record of his egotistical longings, metaphysical aspirations and classicist urges, so in the same way *Trzy zimy* is practically a total record of the consciousness which will give birth to a series of essays, inspired by Maritain's personalism, from the end of the 1930s. If that is not enough, the works published by him in the second half of the interwar period will become a sort of first attempt to codify the views which will be the base of the wartime collection of lyrical poems entitled "Świat (poema naiwne)." Miłosz will write some years later in *Rodzinna Europa* (*Native Realm*) that the astounding cycle of works written during the occupation in search of an alliance of man with apocalyptic reality will be a poetic transformation of reflections born during Father Lallemant's lectures at the Catholic Institute in Paris. It seems that the first such attempt was undertaken by the poet in the middle of the interwar period on the pages of *Trzy zimy* and in poems scattered about the journals of the day. Already at that time he was searching for an answer to the question of what can be opposed to catastrophe, and he already had a presentiment that it would be given by epistemological and metaphysical reflection.

"It is fed by ignorance, darkness, fairy tales and mystery," wrote Miłosz about his poetry. He was certainly thinking, at the time, of the specific aura of prophetic creativity which develops unusual, mysterious, enigmatic and terrifying images and visions of the approaching catastrophe. This self-characterization, however, implies several more complements: the ignorance of the artist who loses his sense of meaning amidst the destructive phenomena of his epoch; the black of the darkness of the future which carries on its flight through the years an inevitable apocalypse; the fairy tale quality of a myth which promises the presence of some sort of transrational justifications; and the mystery of being which apparently disintegrates under its own pressure possesses, nevertheless, its justification in the Absolute.

Notes

1. Prior to its publication in Polish as "Apokalipsa według Czesława Miłosza," Prace Literackie XXVI, Acta Universitatis Wratislaviensis (Wrocław: 1986) this article was submitted for inclusion in this book. It was translated from Polish, including the quotations in the text cited in the notes, by Allan Reid.
2. For the original see S. Napierski, "Czesław Miłosz: '*Trzy zimy,*'"*Ateneum,* nr. 1 (1938), p. 167.
3. For the original see ibid.
4. For the original see A. Fiut, "Czy tylko katastrofizm. O przedwojennej poezji Czesława Miłosza," *Pamiętnik Literacki,* z. 3 (1978), pp. 105–6.
5. For the original see F. Tomaszewski, "Odgarniając pianę odnowień, cóż poczniesz?" *Poezja,* nr. 5/6 (1981), p. 201.
6. Ibid., p. 202.
7. Cz. Miłosz, "Brama wieczoru," *Marchołt,* nr. 3 (1937), p. 354.
8. For the original see Cz. Miłosz, "Wiersze I–V," *Pion,* nr. 16 (1937).
9. For the original see G. Herling-Grudziński, "Granice poezji Miłosza," *Pion,* nr. 8 (1938), pp. 3–4.
10. For the original see Fiut, "Czy tylko katastrofizm," pp. 78–79.
11. For the original see H. Vogler, "Poezja podwójnego oblicza," in *Z notatek przemytnika* (Warsaw: Państwowy Instyut Wydawniczy, 1957), p. 149.

12. For the original see Herling-Grudziński "Granice poezji Miłosza," pp. 3–4.
13. For the original see Napierski, "Czesław Miłosz: '*Trzy zimy*,'" p. 167.
14. For the original see J. Błoński, "Aktualność i trwałość," *Miesięcznik Literacki*, nr. 1 (1974), p. 42.
15. Miłosz, "Brama wieczoru," p. 354.
16. For the original see Fiut, "Czy tylko katastrofizm," p. 97.
17. Cz. Miłosz, "Dytyramb," *Ateneum*, nr. 2 (1938).
18. For the original see Napierski, "Czesław Miłosz: '*Trzy zimy*,'" p. 167.
19. For the original see R. Barthes, "Mit dzisiaj" in *Mit i znak. Eseje* (Warsaw: 1970), p. 58.
20. For the original see M. Eliade, *Sacrum, mit, historia. Wybór esejów* (Warsaw: 1970), p. 116.
21. For the original see P. Kuncewicz, "'Przymierze z ziemią' jako kategoria poetycka drugiej awangardy" in *Z problemów literatury polskiej XX wieku. Literatura międzywojenna*," T. 2 (Warsaw: 1965), p. 166.
22. For the original see ibid., p. 159.
23. For the original see Eliade, *Sacrum, mit, historia*, p. 116.
24. For the original see Cz. Miłosz, "Granice sztuki" in *Stanisław Ignacy Witkiewicz. Człowiek i twórca*, ed. T. Kotarbiński and J.E. Płomiński (Warsaw: Państwowy Instytut Wydawniczy, 1957), pp. 87–88.
25. For the original see J. Pregerówna, "Poezja po wojnie," *Odrodzenie*, nr. 7 (1947), p. 8.
26. For the original see E. Krasnodębska, "*Ocalenie* Czesława Miłosza," *Płomień*, nr. 7 (1947), p. 214.
27. For the original see L. Fryde, *Życie literackie*, z. 2 (1937), p. 74.
28. For the original see Napierski, "Czesław Miłosz: '*Trzy zimy*,'" p. 166.
29. For the original see M. Podraza-Kwiatkowska, *Symbol i symbolika w poezji Młodej Polski. Teoria i praktyka* (Cracow: 1975), p. 55.
30. For the original see *Podręczna encyklopedia biblijna*, ed. ks. E. Dąbrowski, T.I. Poznań (1959), pp. 72–73.
31. For the original see Podraza-Kwiatkowska, *Symbol i symbolika*, p. 54.
32. For the original see Redakcja, "O znaczeniu symbolu," *Zdrój*, z. 1 (1917), p. 32.
33. For the original see Z. Przesmycki, "Maurycy Maeterlinck" in Podraza-Kwiatkowska, *Symbol i symbolika*, p. 23.
34. For the original see ibid., p. 30.
35. For the original see I. Matuszewski, *Słowacki i nowa szutka (modernizm). Twórczość Słowackiego w świetle poglądów estetyki nowoczesnej. Studium krytyczno-porównawcze* (Warsaw: 1965), p. 275.
36. For the original see *Podręczna encyklopedia biblijna*, p. 346.
37. For the original see Fiut, "Czy tylko katastrofizm," pp. 107.
38. For the original see Cz. Miłosz, "List 1/X 1935 r.," *Środy Literackie*, nr. 5 (1935), p. 14.
39. Cz. Miłosz, "Brama poranku," *Marchołt*, nr. 3 (1937), p. 354.

BOGDAN CZAYKOWSKI

The Idea of Reality in the Poetry of Czesław Miłosz

> Próbowałem zgadnąć inną ziemię i nie mogłem.
> Próbowałem zgadnąć inne niebo i nie mogłem.
> ("Mała Pauza," *UP*, 388)

> I tried hard to imagine another earth and could not.
> I tried hard to imagine another heaven and could not.
> ("A Short Recess," *BW*, 56)

In awarding the Nobel Prize for literature to Czesław Miłosz, the Swedish Academy has recognized the achievement of a poet whose work stands apart from the prevailing currents of modernity. In fact, one could speak of Miłosz as a double exile, an exile from his country, and from his epoch, but then one would have to add that this has only strengthened and made more poignant his resolve to belong to a country more profoundly significant than any single time or place—the country of reality. "And I," wrote Miłosz in 1958, recalling his youthful aspirations, "in setting out on my journey had the hope of discovering the secret formula, which enabled one to penetrate the innermost garden of reality, where the rules of the game would be no longer necessary." It was in the name of this quest that Miłosz has opposed, throughout his literary career, all tendencies which appeared to him to diminish the ability of literature to do justice to all that is.

An immediate heir to avant-garde poetic programmes and techniques of the 1920s, Czesław Miłosz found them too restrictive and too specialized, and called upon Polish poets to return to the poetry of Adam Mickiewicz as a model of style, understandably so, since it was Mickiewicz who once said that "poetry was the foremost of the arts through its scope." "For us," wrote Miłosz years later in his essay on Pasternak, "a lyrical stream, a poetic idiom liberated from the chores of discourse was not enough: the poet should be also a *thinking* creature."

One of the first to reflect in Poland on the implications for literature of the experience of the Second World War, Miłosz nevertheless rejected programmatic anti-poetry, deploring its asceticism, the narrowing of its range, and its lack of "an equilibrium between the sense of tragedy and an affirmation of life." In an essay on Aleksander Wat, Miłosz explained his high regard for Wat's poetry by observing that despite its character of an almost "stenographic record of suffering," it was not nihilistic: "Wat was not a nihilist, i.e. he did not inveigh against the dignity of what exists, revenging himself on it for the fact that the subject (I, we, they) is condemned to suffering." At the same time Miłosz rejected socialist realism, and any subordination of literature to ideology, while remaining deeply dissatisfied with various forms of twentieth century naturalism, arguing that naturalism was based on certain unwarranted assumptions, such as the assumption about "the physiological hopelessness, so to say, of human kind."

At the time of the withdrawal of most poets from the "embarrassment of a near concrete reference," and into the "highest generality of speech," Miłosz has, quite consciously, emphasized in his prose as well as in his poetry the value of historicity, the sense of time and place, and the importance of experience, lamenting the attenuation of the *principium individuationis,* and infusing his poetry with rich historical, topographical and autobiographical detail. He wrote in 1946:

> The greatest trouble with contemporary poetry is what someone has called *peu de realité,* i.e. the tendency to stay in the chalk circle of strictly circumscribed modes of reacting to the world. This should not be confused with "ivory tower" attitudes, "art for art's sake," and the like,

> as the problem is rather one of technique. . . . If describing a blade of grass has become problematical, where is there room for a panorama containing people, animals, dawns and sunsets.

Given such views it is understandable that Miłosz's elective affinities with twentieth century poets should have been few, and a matter of strict choice rather than of *esprit de corps* or of influence. They are also highly revealing.

The two poets who have influenced him perhaps the most, Oscar de Milosz and T.S. Eliot, do not appear to have much in common, at least in a superficial sense, and their influence on Miłosz has been very different in kind. Oscar de Milosz, a Lithuanian-French poet, and Czesław's cousin, has been, as we know, the truly parental figure, initiating the younger Polish poet into the mysteries not only of poetic but also of philosophic lore—and I use the word "mysteries" quite advisedly, and without any ironic connotation. It was largely under the influence of his cousin that Miłosz re-evaluated his early distrust of Romanticism and its mystical tendencies, deepened his sense of alienation, and concluded that "there was something very wrong with contemporary literature and, indeed, with the entire epoch."

T.S. Eliot has primarily influenced, or perhaps accentuated, certain tendencies of Miłosz's poetic technique, such as his search for a polyphonic poetic diction (the fusion of different levels or voices, without the loss of their distinctness and its stylistic function), or his insistence on the value of each verse line, both semantic and poetic, and the crucial role in this respect of syntax: "One recognizes good poetry by being able to detach from a poem one line and appreciate its fulness." No doubt, Eliot's sense of the modern malaise and his religious and metaphysical preoccupations have also had their effect on Miłosz.

The case of W.H. Auden illustrates well Miłosz's ability to learn from others on his own terms. In Auden, Miłosz found a poet unafraid of using his intelligence in verse, but also too fond of playing purely intellectual games:

> In Auden, intellectual acumen is reduced to mere constatation . . . often very witty. The author understands so much, that each of his theses is demolished by its antithesis and the result is stasis. This . . . evokes a negative reaction in a European, for whom the world is a dramatic place, and its reduction to purely intellectual equations, from which not only

passion, but even the image of passion, has been eliminated, becomes an offence to human feelings.

Another poet who helped to clarify Miłosz's own view of things at a time when he was seeking again (ten years after his first stay in America) to come to grips with American reality, was Robinson Jeffers. It was typical of Miłosz that he should have turned to the work of a poet as a way of placing himself, or, to use a word Miłosz borrowed from his cousin and made very much his own, of *situating* himself in California, which became his permanent home after 1960. No less typical was the way in which his confrontation which Jeffers's poetry produced a double effect, of rejection as well as of appropriation:

> When I came to California, I devoted considerable time to the poetry of Jeffers. He is, in my view, a very remarkable poet. . . . He consciously opposed avant-garde fashions originating in French symbolism and using proper, transparent syntax, described what had been to him most real, the shores of the Pacific close to his home at Carmel. And yet, in reading Jeffers, I discovered that those orange-violet sunsets, those flights of pelicans, those fishing boats in the morning mist, so faithfully depicted, are like photographs, that all this is for me a fiction, and that Jeffers who subscribed to what he himself had called *inhumanism*, took shelter in an artificial world, which he constructed on a conceptual basis borrowed from biology textbooks and from Nietzsche.

Yet what appeared to Miłosz as Jeffers's unreality had an aspect which served to evaluate a feature of Slavic poetry (and especially of Polish poetry) which Miłosz found both a weakness and an attraction:

> Jeżeli nie czytałeś słowiańskich poetów
> to i lepiej. Nie ma tam czego szukać
> irlandzko-szkocki wędrowiec. Oni żyli w dzieciństwie
> przedłużanym z wieku w wiek. Słońce dla nich było
> rumianą twarzą rolnika, miesiąc patrzył zza chmury
> i Droga Mleczna radowała jak wysadzany brzozami trakt.
>
> ("Do Robinsona Jeffersa," WSF, 74)

> If you have not read the Slavic poets
> so much the better. There's nothing there

for a Scotch-Irish wanderer to seek. They lived in a childhood
prolonged from age to age. For them, the sun
was a farmer's ruddy face, the moon peeped through a cloud
and the Milky Way gladdened them like a birch-lined road.
("To Robinson Jeffers," *SP*, 93)

The reality of Jeffers has helped to throw into relief the unreality of "the Slavic poets," while remaining unacceptable to Miłosz, for reasons clearly spelled out in the poem "Do Robinsona Jeffersa,"

A jednak nie wiedziełeś co wiem. Ziemia uczy
więcej niż nagość żywiołów. Nie daje się sobie
bezkarnie oczu boga. Tak mężny, w pustce,
składałeś ofiary demonom. . . .
. . . .

Raczej wyrzeźbić słońca na spojeniach krzyża
jak robili w moim powiecie. Brzozom i jedlinom
nadawać żeńskie imiona. Wzywać opieki
przeciwko niemej i przebiegłej sile
niż tak jak ty oznajmiać nieczłowieczą rzecz.
("Do Robinsona Jeffersa," *WSF*, 75)

And yet you did not know what I know. The earth teaches
more than does the nakedness of elements. No one with impunity
gives to himself the eyes of a god. So brave, in a void
you offered sacrifices to demons:
. . . .

Better to carve suns and moons on the joints of crosses
as was done in my district. To birches and firs
give feminine names. To implore protection
against the mute and treacherous might
than to proclaim, as you did, an inhuman thing.
("To Robinson Jeffers," *SP*, 94)

Miłosz's sense of his isolation, or at least of his apartness, within the context of poetic modernity, has made him very sensitive to poetic phenomena which appeared to confirm the road he chose to travel. His critical writings are thus not only polemical, but aim at establishing a context for his kind of poetry and vision (and this is also reflected in his wide-ranging activity as a translator of poetry into Polish). Though an admirer of Pasternak, Miłosz ended his important essay on his writings with a clear statement of preference: "From what I have said about my generation's quarrel with worshippers of 'Life,' it should be obvious that Mandelstam, not Pasternak, is for me the ideal of a modern classical poet." The discovery of Cavafy, via English translations, led almost immediately to a presentation of some of his poems in Polish translation (1961), with a characteristic appropriation of Cavafy as an ally: "I have become acquainted with Cavafy's poems very recently. . . . I greeted him like an old acquaintance. After all, we welcome warmly anyone who confirms us in our ways."

Aleksander Wat, a Polish poet whom Miłosz befriended and brought over to Berkeley, became, as we have seen, another ally, and for a number of reasons. Here was a poet whom Mayakovsky had apparently called "a born Futurist," and whose poetry was, without doubt, very modern, but who, nevertheless, was an example of some of the things very dear to Miłosz's heart:

> These poems of Wat . . . fascinate the young people in Berkeley and San Francisco, because they are *zany*. . . . In reality, however, these young readers are attracted by something which is rather rare in the sad buffoonery of contemporary *zany* literature—what attracts them is the weight of content, the interest on the experienced truth.

Another feature which made Wat's poetry close to Miłosz's heart was its range, "from the laments of a biblical prophet to the nearly mathematical wit of gnomic maxims." "Wat," wrote Miłosz, "strove to give poetry a greater scope, the scope which was being destroyed both by the 'purity' of the lyric as well as by verbosity."

It has been suggested that Miłosz's opposition to various modern trends has been, at least to some extent, a matter of an unusual degree of provincialism in a writer deeply attached to the country of his birth, and its vanished world, and that this attachment has engendered in his outlook and poetics a streak of anachronistic passeism. The attachment is certainly there, nevertheless Miłosz's anti-modernism has been a matter of a consistent, if complex, and constantly tested poetic programme, whose cornerstone has been the "worship" of reality. In this programme there was room for a recognition that "what the supporters of an indefinable realism regard as the fault of modern art is often precisely an attempt to capture the maximum of reality or life, with the superficial means discarded," as he put it *à propos* of Saint-John Perse (a view he illustrated elsewhere with reference to Kafka). At the same time "the will to reality" evident in the nineteenth century realist novel has always remained for Miłosz a model of literature performing its proper task, the task of *mimesis.* In the essay entitled "Rzeczywistość" ("Reality") in *Ogród nauk* (Garden of Knowledge), Miłosz quotes with approval Erich Auerbach's observation (from the final chapter of *Mimesis*), to the effect that in modern novels, as well as in other forms of modern art "there is often something confusing, hazy . . . something hostile to the reality which they represent"; that one discerns in them "a vague indefinability of meaning" due to "uninterpretable symbolism." Miłosz's own writings abound in similar observations. Modern poetry, he wrote, has shown itself "increasingly powerless in the face of what reveals itself to us as reality, changing into a self-sufficient activity of language, into *écriture.*" "In my constant encounters with the poetry [of the last quarter of the century in America, Britain and France] I observe . . . that only rarely do I find in it what I myself regard as reality. . . ." "There occurs as if a race between an increasingly irreal language and an increasingly mute reality." "I suspect that the contemporary tendency to seek refuge in linguistic matter as in a system of mirrors, of purely literary reference, springs from the fact that reality appears to have become too difficult." Quotations expressing similar sentiments could be multiplied at will.

In the end, Miłosz's youthful desire to discover a "secret formula" that would enable him to penetrate the innermost garden of reality, while allowing him to dispense with the rules of the game (such, for instance, as the use of language), proved difficult, indeed, close to impossible. The hoped for illumination seemed to remain "for ever potential," beginnings of a revelation seemed never to go beyond the beginning, what initially seemed only a "preface to something else," a kind of "in the meantime" proved "never, even later" to have been "anything but a preface, anything but in the meantime." At the same time, the quest resulted in various formulations of the rules of the game, whose most balanced expression is found in Miłosz's lecture given at Berkeley in 1980, and entitled "O niewiedzy uczonej i literackiej" ("On Ignorance, Learned and Literary"):

> Two basic tendencies may be observed in the poetry of our century: first, a movement from a chaos of images attacking the mind, toward their distillation and such a selection, that they serve one aim only, purity of intonation. And second, an anxiety when form has already

erected a barrier between the raw material of life and arrangements of words, thence immediately a reverse movement, to the point of passively receiving everything which flows in from outside. It is probably in those rare cases when these two tendencies clash within a poem and attain a sort of equilibrium, that durable works are written.

There are, in Miłosz's latest poems dark and powerful expressions of defeat, of disillusionment:

> Stary człowiek, wzgardliwy, czarnego serca,
> Zdumiony, że tak niedawno był dwudziestoletni,
> Mówi.
> A chciałby nie mówić, rozumieć.
>
> Kochał i pragnął, ale nie na dobre wyszło.
> Gonił i prawie chwytał, ale świat był prędszy od niego.
> I teraz widzi złudzenie.
>
> W snach biegnie, mały, po ciemnym ogrodzie.
> Jest tam jego dziadek, ale nie ma gruszy tam gdzie być powinna,
> I furtka otwiera się na gwałtowną falę.
>
> Nieprzebłagana ziemia.
> Niecofnięte prawo.
> Światło nieodkryte.
> ("Osobny zeszyt: przez galerie luster," *SN*, 18)

> An old man, contemptuous, black-hearted,
> Amazed that he was twenty such a short time ago,
> Speaks.
> Though he would rather understand than speak.
>
> He loved and desired, but it turned out badly.
> He pursued and almost captured, but the world was faster than he was.
> And now he sees the illusion.
>
> In his dreams he is running through a dark garden.
> His grandfather is there but the pear tree is not where it should be,
> And the little gate opens to a breaking wave.

Inexorable earth.
Irrevocable law.
The light unyielding.
("The Separate Notebooks: A Mirrored Gallery," *SN*, 19)

Nevertheless, the pithy verdict, contained in the last lines of the quotation, is far from being the whole truth about the results of Miłosz's pilgrimage. For even if it did not happen in the hypothetical way he described in "Gdzie wschodzi słońce i kędy zapada" ("From Where the Sun Rises to Where It Sets"):

Kto raz jedyny rodzi się na ziemi
Mógłby być tym, którego we śnie nawiedziła Isis.
I poddać się obrzędowi wtajemniczenia,
I później mówić: widziałem.
("Mała pauza," *UP*, 387)

Whoever is born just once on earth
Could have been that man whom Isis visited in a dream
And have gone through an initiation
To say afterwards I saw.
("A Short Recess," *BW*, 55)

—yet there is no denying that Miłosz's poetry and his other writings constitute a major, and in many respects a fascinating attempt to grasp and to understand what is real in the life of someone who "is born just once on earth."

"It takes a masterpiece," wrote John Bayley of Miłosz's novel *Dolina Issy (The Issa Valley)* "to reveal the sheer unreality of our modern creative modes and poses." But what does it mean for a twentieth century poet to be a worshipper of reality? Bayley points to one characteristic of Miłosz as a writer, "something in his work that is unique today: the reality of the *thing*, the return of the *thing*." Bayley's observation is, of course, absolutely correct: Miłosz's poetry not only recognizes the reality of the thing, but it consciously attempts to strengthen the ontological status of quiddity in accordance with *principium individuationis*, and despite the knowledge that

Nie wstępuje się dwa razy w to samo jezioro
Po dnie wysłanym olchowymi liśćmi
Łamiąc jedną wąską pręgę słońca.
("Elegia dla N.N.," *UP*, 336)

One cannot step twice into the same lake
on rotting alder leaves,
breaking a narrow sunstreak.
("Elegy for N.N.," *SP*, 96)

Nevertheless, lakes for Miłosz do have their separate existence, as did once a certain "calamus by the river with its scent," however much it was his "alone, and for no one else." Miłosz's poetry is punctuated by such epiphanies of quiddity:

Więc starszy pastuch, skierdź, i torby jego
I chodaki z rzemieniem i najdłuższe biczysko.
Jak też dwóch niedorostków. Jeden ma trąbę brzozową,
Drugi skądś wywlókł sznurkiem związany pistolet.
Rzeczywiście widziani. Koło Szyrwint albo Grynkiszek.
("Nad miastami," *UP*, 383)

So, here is the eldest shepherd and his bags,
And his cross-gartered legs and the longest whipstock.
Two striplings with him. One is carrying a birch-bark trumpet,
The other an old-fashioned pistol, its barrel fixed with a string.
Really seen. Near Širvintai or Grinkiškai.
("Over Cities," *BW*, 51)

Things really seen, touched, smelled, heard, tasted are celebrated, set apart from each other in their distinctness, with the poet's consciousness busily "gathering into a green box specimens of the Earth," choke-cherries, sequoias, jays "with their wings the colour of indigo," "the scent of smoke, of late autumn dahlias on the sloping little streets of a wooden town," "a melody of a mouth organ from afar," dawns, sunsets, a fox

Nie ogólny, pełnomocnik idei lisa w płaszczu podbitym
uniwersaliami.

Ale on, mieszkaniec kamienistych jelniaków niedaleko wioski Żegary.
("Na trąbach i na cytrze," *UP*, 299)

Not a general one, a plenipotentiary of the idea of the fox, in his cloak lined with the universals,
But he, from a coniferous forest near the village of Żegary . . .
("With Trumpets and Zithers," *SP*, 124)

A glossary of concrete nouns in Miłosz's poetry would reveal a passion for the body of the world unmatched in modern poetry, and constantly spurred on not only by an unquenchable appetite, Eros, and the acute sense of flux and changeability, but also by the desire to counteract the dematerialization of the modern mind:

Z drzew, polnych kamieni, nawet cytryn na stole
Uciekła materialność i widmo ich
Okazywało się pustką, dymem na kliszy.
Wydziedziczona z przedmiotów mrowiła się przestrzeń.
("Oeconomia divina," *UP*, 330)

Out of the trees, field stones, even lemons on the table
materiality escaped and their spectrum
proved to be a void, a haze on film
Dispossessed of its objects, space was swarming.
("Oeconomia divina," *SP*, 106)

Yet to limit the significance of Miłosz's poetry to the fact that it counteracts "the disappearance of physical realities from literature" by reinstating in it the reality of the thing, would be to reduce its multidimensionality, taut with the tension of admitted, and often unresolved contradictions, to one level only. It is an important level, for it calls, although indirectly, for the recognition of the validity of the human dimension, the reality of the world as it appears *grosso modo,* as it is given through the senses in a Newtonian rather than Einsteinian space; but it is only one aspect of Miłosz's idea of reality.

The passage quoted above from the poem "Oeconomia divina" about the disappearance of materiality from things, considering that it occurs in a poem with typical North American realia ("Roads of concrete pillars, cities of glass and cast-iron, airfields larger than tribal dominions"), might very well sound ironic, considering the materialism of modern civilization, of the great age, as it appeared to some only very recently, of the fulfillment of the acquisitive instinct. The true dimension of Miłosz's lament over the dematerialization of objects reveals itself when the lines are placed back in their larger context:

Drogom na betonowych słupach, miastom ze szkła i żeliwa,
Lotniskom rozleglejszym niż plemienne państwa
Nagle zabrakło zasady i rozpadły się.
Nie w śnie ale na jawie, bo sobie odjęte
Trwały jak trwa to tylko, co trwać nie powinno.
Z drzew, polnych kamieni, nawet cytryn na stole
Uciekła materialność i widmo ich
Okazywało się pustką, dymem na kliszy.
Wydziedziczona z przedmiotów mrowiła się przestrzeń.
Wszędzie było nigdzie i nigdzie, wszędzie.
Litery ksiąg srebrniały, chwiały się i nikły.
Ręka nie mogła nakreślic znaku palmy, znaku rzeki, ni znaku ibisa.

. . . .

Za mało uzasadnione
Były praca i odpoczynek
I twarz i włosy i biodra
I jakiekolwiek istnienie.

("Oeconomia divina," *UP*, 330)

Roads of concrete pillars, cities of glass and cast-iron,
airfields larger than tribal dominions,
suddenly ran short of their principle and disintegrated.
Not in a dream, but really, for from themselves subtracted,
they could only hold on as do things which should not last.
Out of trees, field stones, even lemons on the table
materiality escaped and their spectrum
proved to be a void, a haze on a film.
Dispossessed of its objects, space was swarming.
Everywhere was nowhere and nowhere, everywhere.
Letters in books turned silver-pale, wobbled and faded.
The hand was not able to trace the palm sign, the river sign, or the
  sign of ibis.

. . . .
Both work and leisure
Were not justified enough,
nor the face, nor the hair nor the loins
nor any existence.

("Oeconomia divina," *SP*, 106)

The thought expressed in these lines is a complex one. Reality, as understood by Miłosz, seems to be as much a matter of things as of their principle, as much physical as social and metaphysical.

In *Rodzinna Europa (Native Realm)*, Miłosz recounts a moment of exceptional ontological intensity:

> Lying in the field near a highway bombarded by airplanes, I riveted my eyes on a stone and two blades of grass in front of me. Listening to the whistle of a bomb, I suddenly understood the value of matter: that stone and those two blades of grass formed a whole kingdom, an infinity of forms, shades, textures, lights. They were the universe . . . I saw into the depths of matter with exceptional intensity.
>
> (*NR*, 204)

The experience was perhaps the birth of the ontological theme in Miłosz's poetry, which has reached its distillation much later, in poems such as "Esse":

> Na to mi przyszło, że po tylu próbach nazywania świata umiem już tylko powtarzać w kółko najwyższe, jedyne wyznanie, poza które żadna moc nie może sięgać: ja *jestem*—ona *jest*. Krzyczcie, dmijcie w trąby, utwórzcie tysiączne pochody, skaczcie, rozdzierajcie sobie ubrania, powtarzając to jedno: *jest!*
>
> ("Esse," *UP*, 207)

> And so it befell me that after so many attempts at naming the world, I am able only to repeat, harping on one string, the highest, the unique avowal beyond which no power can attain: *I am, she is.* Shout, blow the

trumpets, make thousands-strong marches, leap, rend your clothing, repeating only: *is!*

("Esse," *SN*, 7)

This is the fundamental condition, the *sine qua non*, psychological as well as epistemological, of worshipping reality, the fact and the wonder of existence. Without it, and not in theoretical terms but in the sense of the acutest realization of there being existence, the world becomes spectral, like "a haze on a film." The experience can occur at various levels, from the level of metaphysical wonder:

I wznosiło się dalej drzewo niedosiężne.
O iste, o istliwe aż do rdzenia. Było.

("Gucio zaczarowany," *UP*, 256)

And still there stood the tree unattainable.
O veritable, o true to the very core. It was.

("Bobo's Metamorphosis," *SP*, 103)

to the level of animal-like sensation:

Gdybym miał przedstawić czym jest dla mnie świat
wziąłbym chomika albo jeża albo kreta,
posadziłbym go na fotelu wieczorem w teatrze
i przytykając ucho do mokrego pyszczka
słuchałbym co mówi o świetle reflektorów,
o dźwiękach muzyki i ruchach baletu.

("Po ziemi naszej," *UP*, 241)

If I had to tell what the world is for me,
I would take a hamster or a hedgehog or a mole
and place him in a theatre seat one evening
and bringing my ear to his humid snout,
would listen to what he says about the spotlights,
sounds of music, and movements of the dance.

("Throughout Our Lands," *SP*, 81)

This level, however, is also very important, especially to a poet, since to be a poet means "to approach the mystery of existence more directly than through mere concepts." In other words, to be a poet means, for Miłosz, to penetrate to reality through conceptual haze, and, as he has suggested on a number of occasions, through the haze of modern sophistication.

Not being a philosopher in the more technical sense of the term, Miłosz does not provide us in his works with a definition or a theory of reality. His philosophical erudition is undoubtedly wide, but his readings in philosophy have been, if we may draw conclusions from the somewhat cryptic discussion of this point in the book by A. Fiut, *Rozmowy z Czesławem Miłoszem* (Conversations with Czesław Miłosz), published in Cracow in 1981, both unsystematic and very selective. Typical of his philosophical attitude is the poem "Sroczość" ("Magpiety"), in which we read:

> Kto by pomyślał, że, tak, po stuleciach,
> Wynajdę spór o uniwersalia.
>
> ("Sroczość," *UP*, 209)

> Who would have guessed that, centuries later,
> I would invent again the dispute over universals?
>
> ("Magpiety," *SP*, 20)

The attitude that as a thinker he is "the same kind of a philosopher as everybody else" has freed Miłosz from the straitjacket of epistemological doubt or overawed reverence. "Let us say," he tells his interviewer, Aleksander Fiut, when pressed, "that my philosophizing is analogous to the situation of Mr. Jourdain, who did not know that he spoke prose." And when pressed further, this time in connection with Witold Gombrowicz, Miłosz makes a statement in Fiut's book which is almost nonchalant in its offhandedness:

> For Gombrowicz the world always exists here, in the head. We cannot say anything about the existence or nonexistence of the world. Gombrowicz's standpoint is thus, to be sure, very sceptical. As for me, I have always, I don't know why, in a sort of impulsive way, taken the side of extreme realism. Even as far as the realism of St. Thomas Aquinas. There is horseness, and there is a horse. The latter is a realization of the former. But I am not saying this too seriously.

Miłosz's preference as a thinker is to be as much as possible on his own and to draw from philosophical writings only that which seems to confirm his own insights and ideas, as when he quotes in the prose-and-verse poem

"Osobny zeszyt" ("The Separate Notebooks"), a passage from Schopenhauer, whose main point throws an interesting light on Miłosz's preoccupation with things:

> ... jeżeli więc przedmiot do tego stopnia wykroczył poza wszelkie związki z czymkolwiek poza nim, a podmiot poza wszelkie związki z wolą, wtedy co tak poznajemy, nie jest już poszczególną rzeczą, ale Ideą, formą wieczną, bezpośrednią obiektywizacją woli na tym szczeblu;
>
> ("Obsobny zeszyt: przez galerie luster," *SN*, 40)

> ... if thus the object has to such an extent passed out of all relation to the will, then that which is so known is no longer the particular thing as such; but it is the *idea*, the eternal form, the immediate objectivity of the will at this grade. . . .
>
> ("The Separate Notebooks: A Mirrored Gallery," *SN*, 41)

prefacing the entire, rather abstruse and difficult passage, with the words: "And I concede, your words confirmed what I had experienced myself" (*SN*, 41).

Characteristically, Miłosz does not say "what I have thought myself," he juxtaposes to the thought of the philosopher what he calls his experience. And this is precisely his way, to trust his own experience, his insights, while taking umbrage behind a philosophical naivete which a poet may be excused for assuming if only for the reason that he tries "to approach the mystery of existence more directly than through mere concepts." Such umbrage is taken by Miłosz in his polemic with bishop Berkeley in the poem "Nadzieja" ("Hope") in the sequence of poems significantly entitled "Świat (poema naiwne)" ("The World (A Naive Poem)"):

> Niektórzy mówią, że nas oko łudzi
> I że nic nie ma, tylko się wydaje,
> Ale ci właśnie nie mają nadziei.
> Myślą, że kiedy człowiek się odwróci,
> Cały świat za nim zaraz być przestaje,
> Jakby porwały go ręce złodziei.
>
> ("Nadzieja," *UP*, 90)

> Some people think our eyes deceive us; they say
> That there is nothing but a pretty seeming:

And just these are the ones who don't have hope.
They think that when a person turns away
The whole world vanishes behind his back
As if a clever thief had snatched it up.

("Hope," *SN*, 145)

If the argument does not quite do justice to Berkeley's subtle position, it does seem efficacious against those who draw from philosophy unwarranted or naive conclusions. That there is strength to be found in rejecting sophistication which seems to go against the grain of reasonableness and experience is shown again by Miłosz in his Nobel Lecture, where we read:

> I give to this word reality its naive and solemn meaning, a meaning having nothing to do with philosophical debates of the last few centuries. It is the Earth as seen by Nils from the back of the gander and by the author of the Latin ode from the back of Pegasus.[1] Undoubtedly, the Earth *is* and her riches cannot be exhausted by any description. To make such an assertion means to reject in advance a question we often hear today, "What is reality?", for it is the same as the question of Pontius Pilate: "What is truth?". If among pairs of opposites which we use every day the opposition of life and death has such an importance, no less importance should be ascribed to the oppositions of truth and falsehood, or reality and illusion.

There is thus more than a hint in Miłosz that it is better not to try to ask such questions, than to err on the side of Pontius Pilate, a strange and unsavoury parallel for those philosophers who had insisted on asking precisely such questions, though not necessarily with the same intention.

"Reality gets along without definition" we read in the lecture "O niewiedzy uczonej i literackiej," which also contains the most explicit statement of Miłosz's strategy in his opposition to the hallmarks of modern thought:

> We are born only once on this earth and are given only one historical time, and not any other. If we are aware of living by chance in a decadent epoch, then we are faced with the question of the choice of tactics. Since man is not an animal, and is in touch with the entire past of his kind. . . . he cannot but get depressed that instead of trying to equal the greatest human accomplishments, we submit to inferior philosophies,

> only because they are contemporary. Finding the right tactics of resistance is quite difficult and our development, worthy of the name, should probably move from an unconscious to a conscious tactics. Unfortunately, the individual, subjected to the same influences as those around him, is weak and constantly ponders if it is not he who is wrong.
>
> [tr. B.C.]

Convinced that he is right, yet full of doubt, Miłosz nevertheless does tackle the question of defining reality more directly in some of his later essays. In the essay from which I have just quoted, he says that "in its most general sense, reality is all that which surrounds man on account of his being born in a certain place and at a certain time. There was a time when that meant a village, a city, a country. Today it is the evolving history of the entire globe." In his essay 'Rzeczywistość" ("Reality"), Miłosz elaborates and clarifies. He notes that in popular usage the word means "all the things which act according to their laws, and in such a way that if we find ourselves on the course along which they are moving, we perish." And since the thing that threatens us more than the physical world is another man, reality, argues Miłosz, is first and foremost social, i.e., "one in which men-things carry out orders given by other men, who act as if they were masters of their own and other peoples' fate, but in truth are also transformed into things by the so-called necessities of life."

There is another observation that Miłosz ventures directly in this connection, and it is that "all existence within our grasp is hierarchical." He develops this theme by focusing on Dostoyevsky, whose realism, he says, "consciously opposed to the apparent realism of his contemporaries," still preserves its vitality on account of the fact that its essence lies in the "deciphering of signs." For Dostoyevsky, writes, Miłosz, "reality was multilayered, but not all of the layers provided the key to what was of real importance in the 'enormous welter of tangled threads.'" Thus, reality, all that which surrounds us on account of the time and place of our being, is also a matter of man's consciousness, of his ability to perceive its hierarchical nature. Dostoyevsky's greatness as a realist lies, according to Miłosz, in the fact that he was not so much a psychologist, but "as has been rightly pointed out, a pneumatologist, which is something quite different." "Pneuma—spirit, is not the same as the apparatus for recording impressions which is sometimes called the soul, and the struggle for the salvation of men *pneumatikos,* against the temptations of man *psychikos,* is worthy of the highest stakes."

If we now ask why is such a struggle worthy of the highest stakes, the answer will have to be that this is so because reality, for Miłosz, is not only material, physical, and not only social, political, but also metaphysical and religious. A very large part of Miłosz's strategy of development (if that is the best way of describing it), from the unconscious to the more conscious, has been the probing of the religious, theological aspect of reality, both in his prose, and especially in the long essay *Ziemia Ulro (The Land of Ulro)*, and in his poetry, with the tentative and implicit becoming increasingly explicit, as in the major poem "Gdzie wschodzi słońce i kędy zapada" ("From Where the Sun Rises to Where It Sets"), in which there occurs this startlingly forthright confession:

> Należę jednak do tych którzy wierzą w *apokatastasis*.
> Słowo to przyobiecuje ruch odwrotny,
> Nie ten co zastygł w *katastasis*,
> I pojawia się w Aktach Apostolskich, 3, 21.
>
> Znaczy: przywrócenie. Tak wierzyli święty Grzegorz z Nyssy,
> Johannes Scotus Erigena, Ruysbroek i William Blake.
>
> Każda rzecz ma więc dla mnie podwójne trwanie.
> I w czasie i kiedy czasu już nie będzie.
>
> ("Dzwony w zimie," *UP*, 399)

> Yet I belong to those who believe in *apokatastasis*.
> That word promises reverse movement,
> Not the one that was set in *katastasis*,
> And appears in the Acts, 3, 21.
>
> It means: restoration. So believed: St. Gregory of Nyssa,
> Johannes Scotus Erigena, Ruysbroeck and William Blake.
>
> For me, therefore, everything has a double existence.
> Both in time and when time shall be no more.
>
> ("Bells in Winter," *BW*, 69)

Let us note that this concept of the ultimate reality seems especially suitable for a poet so enamoured of individual existences, so meticulous in his desire to strengthen the ontological status of a particular fox "from the coniferous forest near the village of Żegary," someone who wrote that "a word should be contained in every single thing," and who asserted that the mere naming of things could fill one's entire lifetime, viewing such activity as a way of making existence stronger:

> Co jest wymówione wzmacnia się.
> Co nie jest wymówione zmierza do nieistnienia.
> ("Czytając japońskiego poetę Issa," *PIII,* 31)

> What is pronounced strengthens itself.
> What is not pronounced tends to nonexistence.
> ("Reading the Japanese Poet Issa," *SN,* 209)

Among a series of short sententiae or notes (as the Polish term *zdania* has been rendered in English), we find the following, composed as an inscription "to be placed over the unknown grave of L.F.":

> Co było w tobie zwątpieniem, przegrało, co było w tobie wiarą, spełniło się.
> ("Zdania," *P,* 37)

> What was in doubt in you, lost, what was faith in you, triumphed.
> ("Sentences," tr. B.C.)

In the late 1960s and throughout the 1970s, Miłosz's poetry and thought were becoming increasingly religious, one could say theological. The use of the latter term may appear far-fetched: of how many twentieth century poets can it be said that their pursuit of knowledge has led them into this rather specialized area, but then of how many twentieth century poets can it be said that they pursued any kind of knowledge at all. Whatever view is taken of a poetry whose themes overlap with theological concerns, this is precisely the area into which Miłosz's search for illumination, his quest for reality, has increasingly led him, as he has himself recognized. In the introduction to his translation of the *Book of Job,* Miłosz stated that "the central and perhaps the only question" which exercised his mind even before he had become interested in being a writer, was the question of "the evil of the world, of the pain and suffering of living creatures as an argument against God." If "the whole of theology is in the *Book of Job,*" as Miłosz says elsewhere, there is no need to justify further the use of the term with regard to

Miłosz's later pursuits, such as his interest in Simone Weil, Lev Shestov or S. Bulgakov, his translations from the Bible, and the major prose writings of his Californian period, though one may quote the explanation he gave at the Catholic University of Lublin in 1981, when he said that in pursuing these interests he wanted perhaps "to show that such pursuits were not reserved . . . for professional Catholics only."

The theological aspect of Miłosz's idea of reality would require a more extensive treatment than I can provide in this short paper. It comprises Miłosz's gnostic and Manichean tendencies, his firm belief in the existence of good and evil, his conviction that "we walk over hell while looking at flowers," the attempt to find in human history a link between transience and "the eternal moment," the probing of eschatological and apocalyptic ideas and visions, and the polemic with the limiting character of the scientific outlook. In fact Miłosz's prose writings of his Californian period, to mention only *Widzenia nad zatoką San Francisco (Visions from San Francisco Bay)* and *Ziemia Ulro (The Land of Ulro)*, may be viewed as an attempt to create intellectual space for faith as a mode of becoming aware of reality. The opening up of this space had to contend, of course, with modern scepticism, scientism, and the silliness (the term is Miłosz's) of contemporary academic theology. In this attempt we find Miłosz using a variety of approaches, from discursive and dialectical, such as the statement that "piety . . . exists independently of the division into believers and atheists, a division which is, at least today, illusory, considering that faith is undermined by the doubting of faith, and disbelief is undermined by the doubting of disbelief," to parabolic, such as the story of the drowning beetle which Miłosz tried to save unsuccessfully, leading to the observation that "there may be close to me superior creatures of whom I know nothing, just as my presence is unknown to the beetle." It takes the form of evaluating the insights and beliefs of mystical and religious writers, such as Swedenborg, Mickiewicz, Blake, or Oscar de Milosz. It takes the form of disquisitions on the concept of God. But it is only in poetry that we find Miłosz approaching the certainty, the inner conviction of someone who believes. Nowhere in Miłosz's writing do we find expression of the knowledge of supernatural reality as a result of direct, mystical experience and revelation. It is rather that trusting in the poetic mood, he allows himself to assert what he has sought after so diligently, so consistently and what would constitute, if truly found, a knowledge of the real behind the real.

Such poems are rare, interspersed with expressions of bitter doubt and disillusionment, but they speak more strongly in this context. Here belongs "Odległość" ("Distance"), in which God is addressed directly (a most rare occurrence in Miłosz's poetry), though, at the same time, with great circumspection

> W pewnej odległości postępuję za Tobą, wstydząc się podejść bliżej.
> Choć wybrałeś mnie na robotnika Twojej winnicy i tłoczyłem
> grona Twego gniewu.
>
> . . . .
>
> Tak wielu jest dobrych i prawych, ci najsłuszniej byli wezwani
> I gdziekolwiek stąpasz po ziemi, tam idą i towarzyszą.
> Może to prawda, że Ciebie w skrytości kochałem.
> Ale bez wielkiej nadziei, że będę przy Tobie jak oni.
>
> ("Odległość," *PIII*, 50–51)

> I follow You at a certain distance, ashamed to draw near.
> Although You have chosen me to be a labourer in Your vineyard
> and I crushed the grapes of Your wrath.
>
> . . . .
>
> The good and the righteous are many, and they have been called
> justly.
> And wherever you walk on the earth, they follow and accompany
> You.
> Perhaps it is true, that, secretly, I have loved You.
> But without too much hope, that I will be, like they, at Your side.
>
> ("Distance," tr. B.C.)

Here belongs above all else the short masterpiece of Miłosz's religious verse "Do Józefa Sadzika,"[12] ("To Joseph Sadzik"), who had been, until his death in 1980, a close friend of Miłosz's and his collaborator in the translating of the Psalms, the *Book of Job* and other Biblical writings. There is no mention in the poem of the fact that J. Sadzik was a priest, and the reproach for his untimely death is a reproach one makes to a friend for disappearing suddenly, "in the middle of a conversation," and without even saying, "I'll be back." But the personal grief is almost immediately subsumed in a meditation on the nature of the other world. With characteristic forthrightness, Miłosz rejects as unsatisfactory ideas of the other world which divide the living and the dead, separating them by an unbreachable barrier:

Żywi z żywymi zanadto złączeni
Żebym uznawał moc zamkniętych granic
I nad podziemną rzeką, w państwie cieni
Zgodził się ciebie, żywego, zostawić.
("Do Józefa Sadzika," *PIII*, 101)

The living are too closely bound to the living
For me to recognize the power of closed borders,
And to consent to leave you, alive,
By an underground river, in the realm of shadows.
("To Joseph Sadzik," tr. E.M.)

The call for advice and prayer, that is addressed to the departed friend, is thus made in the confidence that he will hear the voice, and as the conviction of the impossibility of final separation grows, the poem bursts into a hymnic last stanza in which faith is momentarily triumphant and the real behind the real is made manifest:

Niech triumfuje Świętych Obcowanie
Oczyszczający ogień, tu i wszędzie,
I co dzień wspólne z martwych powstawanie
Ku Niemu, który jest i był i będzie.
("Do Józefa Sadzika, *PIII*, 101)

Let the Communion of the Saints triumph
And a purifying fire, here and everywhere,
Together with our common rising from the dead
Towards Him, who is, was and will be.
("To Joseph Sadzik," tr. E.M.)

It will be most suitable to conclude with Miłosz's own statement, in which he recollects once more the powerful desire that became his lifelong quest:

> I recognized that reality is a good deal more profound than what I might happen to think about it and that it allows for various types of cognition. . . . Nothing [however] could stifle my inner certainty that a shining point exists where all lines intersect. . . . Time opened up before me

like a fog. If I was worthy enough I would penetrate it, and then I would understand.

Notes

1. Miłosz refers here to the hero of Selma Lagerlöf's novel *The Wonderful Adventure of Nils*, and to Maciej Sarbiewski, a seventeenth-century Polish-Latin poet, known in the rest of Europe under the penname of Casimire.
2. Cz. Miłosz, "Do Józefa Sadzika," *Tygodnik Powszechny* 6 (1981), p. 5.

MADELINE G. LEVINE

Warnings to the West

Czesław Miłosz's Political Prose of the 1950s

A discussion of Czesław Miłosz's political prose[1] of the 1950s must begin by acknowledging that Miłosz himself does not consider these writings to be in the mainstream of his work. "Writing for foreigners," Miłosz has asserted, "was only a pragmatic or even pedagogical undertaking, for I do not believe in the possibility of understanding outside the same language and the same historical tradition."[2] Farther on in the same essay he remarks, "I have actually written only one novel, *The Issa Valley*. . . ."[3]

The first comment incorporates a statement of belief about the impossibility of transnational understanding that can only be noted here, not challenged. The second, however, is simply inaccurate; *The Issa Valley* (1981), originally published in Polish as *Dolina Issy* (1955), is not Miłosz's only novel. There is another novel—a pedagogical, pragmatic work directed primarily at foreigners and first published in French in 1953 under the title *La prise du pouvoir.* Called *Zdobycie władzy* in Polish (in which language it was published in 1953), it is known in English translation as *The Seizure of Power* (1955).[4] Like its companion volumes, *Zniewolony umysl* (1953) *(The*

Captive Mind (1953))[5] and the later *Rodzinna Europa* (1959) (*Native Realm* (1968)),[6] this novel represents Miłosz's attempt to convey to a wider audience—to West European leftists (if they would grant a hearing to this "turncoat")—his bitter findings about Soviet state power and the fateful seductiveness of historical determinism in its Soviet Marxist variant.

The central insights into the relationships between intellectuals and Communism as ideology and as power, which are developed with considerable care in the 1950s in *The Captive Mind, The Seizure of Power,* and *Native Realm,* had already been formulated by Miłosz in the late 1940s. Their first literary expression is in the poetry of *Światło dzienne* (Daily Light), a volume published in 1955, but incorporating poems from the late 1940s. It seems that the political prose of the 1950s does not differ significantly in its basic political insights from such poems as "Dziecię Europy" ("Child of Europe"), and "Traktat moralny" ("Moral Treatise"). I am thinking, for example, of such trenchant lines as the following from "Dziecię Europy":

> Jak należy się ludziom poznaliśmy dobro i zło.
> Nasza złośliwa mądrość nie ma sobie równej na ziemi.
>
> . . . .
>
> Nie może być mowy o triumfie sił
> Bowiem jest to epoka gdy zwycięża sprawiedliwość.
>
> Nie wspominaj o sile, by cię nie posądzono
> Że w ukryciu wyznajesz doktryny upadłe.
>
> Kto ma władzę, zawdzięcza ją logice dziejów.
> Oddaj logice dziejów cześć jej należną.
>
> . . . .
>
> Niech kłamstwo logiczniejsze będzie od wydarzeń,
> Aby znużeni wędrowką znaleźli w nim ukojenie.
>
> Po dniu kłamstwa gromadźmy się w dobranym kole
> Bijąc się w uda ze śmiechu, gdy wspomni kto nasze czyny.
> ("Dziecię Europy," *UP,* 122–24)

> As befits human beings, we explored good and evil
> Our malignant wisdom has no like on this planet.
> . . . .

There can be no question of force triumphant.
We live in the age of victorious justice.

Do not mention force, or you will be accused
Of upholding fallen doctrines in secret.

He who has power, has it by historical logic.
Respectfully bow to that logic.

. . . .

Let your lie be even more logical than the truth itself,
So the weary travelers may find repose in the lie.

After the Day of the Lie gather in select circles,
Shaking with laughter when our real deeds are mentioned.
("Child of Europe," *SP*, 59–62.)

Or consider these warnings from "Traktat moralny":

Bo schizofrenia—rozdwojenie
Istoty na kwiat i korzenie,
Poczucie, że te moje czyny
S p e ł n i a m   n i e   j a,   a l e   k t o ś   i n n y.
Kark skręcić komuś jest drobnostką.
Potem Komedię czytać Boską,
Czy stary oklaskiwać kwartet,
Lub dyskutować awangardę.
Na mniejszą skalę, to codzienne,
Ktoś mówi: zło jest bezimienne,
A nas użyto jak narzędzi.
Ma rację. I ku zgubie pędzi.
("Traktat moralny," *UP*, 151)

There's a schizophrenia or division
of people into roots and fruit,
The feeling that my deeds are done
By someone other than myself.
To bow one's neck is but a trifle,
Then one can read the *Paradiso*,
Applaud a concert of old music,

Appreciate the avantgarde.
In simpler ways this happens daily.
Someone says, "Evil's really nameless,
And we are being used as tools."
He's right. And racing towards destruction.
("Moral Treatise," tr. M.L.)

In short, Miłosz had already concluded that the Communist seduction of intellectuals in Poland, the Baltic states, and elsewhere in Eastern Europe, was based on the comforting lure of an ideology which guaranteed its adherents a place in the triumphant vanguard of History. He was convinced that a people exhausted by their struggle against the Nazi oppressors would delude themselves into believing that there was no chance but to accept Soviet oppression, and would therefore consider themselves morally uncompromised by their acquiescence. According to his testimony in *Native Realm*, Miłosz had explored these ideas in the late 1940s with others, like him, initiated into the dark secrets of political manoeuvering in post-war Eastern Europe. Miłosz switched from verse to prose in the 1950s in an attempt to find a language and a style in which to communicate to the uninitiated—both emigré Poles and Western intellectuals—the insights already distilled in his didactic poems. Driven by a fervent desire to bear witness to the expansionist menace of Soviet Communism, and by what appears to have been an obsessive need to reconstruct his own political/historical identity, Miłosz experimented with delivering his message to the West in three widely differing prose genres: the hybrid philosophical essay/portrait series of *The Captive Mind*; the kaleidoscopic novel, *The Seizure of Power*; and the intellectual/sociological autobiography, *Native Realm*.

Before discussing these three works, it may be useful to review briefly the historical context of Miłosz's life up to the point at which he made his début in the West. In his introduction to *Native Realm* Miłosz describes the genesis of the autobiography, and discusses the distances he has to cross in order to communicate the strange contours of his native region to those for whom it is, at best, only a name on a map:

> The revolving globe of the earth has become very small, and, geographically speaking, there are no longer any uncolored areas on it. In Western Europe, however, it is enough to have come from the largely untraveled territories in the East or North to be regarded as a visitor from Septentrion, about which only one thing is known: it is cold. . . . Undoubt-

> edly I could call Europe my home, but it was a home that refused to acknowledge itself as a whole; instead, as if on the strength of some self-imposed taboo, it classified its population into two categories: members of the family (quarrelsome but respectable) and poor relations. How many times have I remained silent because, having come from those foggy expanses that books, even textbooks, rarely provide information about (or, if they do, provide false), I would have had to start from scratch!... No, I will never imitate those who rub out their traces, disown the past and are dead, although they pretend they are alive with the help of mental acrobatics. My roots are in the East; that is certain. Even if it is difficult or painful to explain who I am, nevertheless I must try.[7]

Miłosz was born in that area of northern Europe which is now part of the Lithuanian Socialist Republic of the USSR. His early childhood, as we learn from *Native Realm*, was marked by the turmoil of the last years of the Russian Empire, the witnessed chaos of war and revolution. His peaceful if impoverished youth, spent in the provincial but culturally heterogeneous city of Wilno—a Polish city during the inter-war years—yielded to a manhood entered upon in the chaotic decade of the 1930s, with its growth of extremist political groups based on ideologies of class and race hatred; the world-wide financial débâcle of "pure" capitalism; and intimations, for those who would see them (and Miłosz was among them) of a coming catastrophic upheaval.

With the outbreak of war on September 1, 1939, this world, shaky beneath its veneer of stability, came crashing down. Polish resistance to the German invasion was swiftly crushed, the final blow being dealt by an invasion from the East—the Red Army occupation of Poland's easternmost territories in accordance with the until then secret accords of the Molotov-Ribbentrop pact.

Polish society disintegrated into chaos. In the East, millions of Polish citizens, caught in their flight from the Nazis, were arrested and transported to the outlying reaches of the Soviet Empire where they languished (if they did not die) until the exigencies of the Soviet war effort after the German invasion of that country in June 1941 resulted in an amnesty and the formation on Soviet territory of two Polish armies—one released to fight with the Allies in Palestine and northern Africa; the other included as a special Polish division within the Red Army. This latter Polish army was eventually used to pave the way for the establishment of Communist power in "liberated" Poland after the defeat of Nazi Germany.

In the parts of Poland either incorporated into the Reich or constituted as the Government General, terror reigned supreme as the Nazis systematically developed their plan of exterminating the large indigenous Jewish population and turning the ethnic Polish population into a subclass of slave labourers. Poland, of course, also was chosen as the location for the vast slave-labour and extermination camps which serviced all of Europe.

Trapped by chance in the Eastern zone, Miłosz made a harrowing illegal crossing back to Warsaw where he spent the war years, devoting himself to literature and the difficult business of daily survival. Like so many returnees from Soviet gulags, Miłosz, in *Native Realm*, speaks of the curious spiritual freedom he discovered during this period of degradation and terror.

The return of peace brought an entirely new set of problems. Poland, freed from her German oppressors, fell directly into the clutches of the expanding Soviet Empire. Although armed resistance to Soviet power continued for another two years or so, the only realistic alternatives for Polish citizens were emigration or grudging acceptance of the new state of affairs. Within the latter alternative there were, to be sure, degrees of accommodation, although for public figures the range of choices might not, in fact, be very broad. Writers, for example, could, in theory at least, defy the ever-increasing censorship and write what they chose, taking all the political risks that entailed; they could institute a form of self-censorship and write or submit for publication only what appeared neutral and acceptable; they could write for the drawer, thereby entering a state of internal emigration; they could fall silent, with the knowledge that in a totalitarian state silence is a suspicious activity; they could become antiquarians, pushing their interests back to politically safe historical periods or, out of similar motives of self protection, they could become translators. They could, finally, raise their voices in support of the Communist regimes, even to the point of writing nauseating odes in praise of the virtues of Joseph Stalin—and they could do so either because they truly believed in what they were writing or because that approach seemed the cleverest way to guarantee survival. If one adds to this the by no means simple tasks of deciding what topics were politically acceptable or desirable, and what were the risks to physical safety and moral self-esteem at any point, one has some idea of the tormenting situation in which the East European intellectuals, like their Soviet counterparts a quarter of a century earlier, now found themselves as their countries moved inexorably towards the establishment of Communist power.

Although Miłosz is by no means the only writer to have described the labyrinth of impossible choices confronting the intellectual under Communist rule, he was one of the first to do so for Eastern Europe as opposed to the Soviet Union. Both in *Native Realm,* where he traces his own manoeuverings as a servant of the regime (cultural attaché to the Polish Embassy in Washington, then in Paris), and in *The Captive Mind,* where he analyses the trap in which the Polish writers were caught and subjects four readily identifiable specimens to his dissecting scalpel, Miłosz insists that the East European situation was not strictly comparable to the Soviet one.

Contrary to what his anti-Communist readers may have thought, the East European intellectuals who accepted the Communist system, Miłosz contends, were not simply self-serving. They had emerged from the War with an intimate knowledge of evil and a heavy burden of guilt, for it had been impossible to be always "heroic" or always virtuous in the face of annihilating power. They were familiar with the treachery of History, the instability of so-called normal life. As Miłosz writes in *The Captive Mind:* "Whoever has not dwelt in the midst of horror and dread cannot know how strongly a witness and a participant protests against himself, against his own neglect and egoism. Destruction and suffering are the school of social thought."[8]

The burden of Miłosz's argument in *The Captive Mind* and in parts of *Native Realm* which are devoted to the post-war period is that the Communist menace (to borrow a phrase from the Cold War years in which these works were written) is real and dangerous, and one of its more curious features is that it may attract adherents of considerable moral and intellectual perspicacity who acknowledge that menace but perceive cooperation with it as a cunning if dangerous contest with History.

In his essay on "ketman" which opens *The Captive Mind,* Miłosz argues that by virtue of their mental suppleness intellectuals are peculiarly susceptible to moral self-destruction. He calls this "ketman." The reasoning of "ketman," a concept found in Islam, goes like this: If I find myself in an untenable position because of my faith, it is perfectly consistent with my faith to deny it publicly so long as I preserve that faith as a matter of private conscience, no matter how long this situation may continue. Miłosz suggests that "ketman" provides a perfect analogy for the thinking of intellectuals in Eastern Europe who decided to engage in the game of pretending to support fully the emerging Communist regimes while priding themselves on their internal moral and intellectual reservations. Such a game with the powers that be might be entered upon for a number of reasons, among them: the sheer sport of the enterprise, with its delicious dose of danger; doubts about the justice of opposing the laws of History embodied in the victorious forces of Soviet Communism; a sincere belief that the struggle against Communism was so important that it was far better to remain alive until such time as opposition might reasonably be judged feasible than to risk losing by a rash stand on principle even one sorely needed supporter of one's true cause. All of these positions rest on the belief that, at the present moment, Communism *is* History's anointed movement, for good or for bad, and that the other political and class forces in the world are clearly bankrupt and defeated—or, at the very least, uninterested in the fate of the millions of people of Central Europe and the Baltics.

In the last two chapters of *Native Realm*, which are devoted to "Tiger," —Miłosz's code name for his philosopher-friend who began as an opponent of the Communists and ended as a professor of philosophy at the Party School in Warsaw—Miłosz reveals his own flirtation with "ketman." For a while he sought to serve the new state as a diplomat, justifying his position by the belief that "it was we who were really changing the world, slyly, patiently, from within; we were the worm in the apple."[9] Assignment abroad won him a degree of freedom from the state's ideological watchdogs, and allowed him to write poems which he could not write at home, some of which were actually published in Poland. However, as the net of compromise grew tighter, Miłosz had doubts about the possibility of any individual winning in this game of inner opposition. Eventually, the decisive factor in his decision to break off the game and go into self-imposed exile was the formal imposition of the restrictive rules of Socialist Realism on Polish literature. Tiger, who originally argued against Miłosz's cooperation with the Communists and ended by joining their camp, stands as a pitiful warning to those who think "ketman" can be practised for an extended period without moral damage. Miłosz defends Tiger as someone who may have chosen to side with evil but did not do so blindly, and who took upon himself the agony of upholding a cause and an ideology despite his clear awareness of their many flaws. Miłosz writes about his relationship with Tiger:

> First Tiger had been in the Western camp and I in the Eastern, then both of us in the Eastern, and now our positions were reversed completely.... We were only intellectuals, who always deceive the prince in

> power because his goal is never their goal. And even if our outer successes have sometimes been enviable, our lot in this century of conformity is the worst of all.[10]
>
> . . . .
>
> [Tiger] joked that Hegel was so difficult he had made him sick. His joke was, I think, more of a confession than anyone realized. Tiger was killed by his game. The heart, too quickly consumed by the game, is unable to keep up with the mind, straining to discern the will of God in the current of history.[11]

The danger of this game is described in simpler terms in *The Seizure of Power.* The mother of Piotr Kwinto, one of the novel's central characters, warns her son, who is confronted by many of the ethical dilemmas described by Miłosz as his own: "It will be an abyss, without anything to cling to. . . . What begins as a lie will remain a lie. . . . Whoever speaks the way he has to will begin to think the way he has to."[12]

In *The Captive Mind* Miłosz offers four portraits of writers who experimented with either "ketman" or dialectical reasoning. Called "Alpha," "Beta," "Gamma," and "Delta" in the book, they are easily identifiable as well-known Polish literary figures. "Gamma" (Jerzy Putrament) is the simplest; a not very talented man, he needed power and official busyness to distract him from his failures as a writer. He gave his loyalty to the Party, which in return declared him superior to his more talented literary peers. Eventually he became head of the Writers' Union—a sinister position in Stalinist Poland.

"Delta" (Konstanty Ildefons Gałczyński), a brilliant and irreverent poet whom Miłosz portrays as a cross between a court jester and a troubadour, was a drunken buffoon who reveled in shocking behaviour and sold his verse to whoever was in a position to pay for it. He had few moral scruples, held the bourgeoisie in contempt, and despite or because of his irreverent sense of humour, had little trouble producing ecstatic poems in praise of Stalin and the Soviet utopia—poems so extravagantly enthusiastic that perhaps they were an exercise in the spirit of "ketman."

"Beta" (Tadeusz Borowski) was the youngest of the four. He had blossomed as a poet of great promise during the first years of the Occupation, was arrested and sent to Auschwitz, and emerged from that dread extermination camp filled with hatred and poised to bear witness against the concentration camp universe and the social order that had spawned it. Borowski's stories about Auschwitz are recognized by almost everyone who deals with the subject of concentration camp literature as models of what such literature can, and perhaps should, be like. But this hatred drove "Beta" to serve the exterminating power of the Revolution, and he dedicated his enormous talents to the production of polemical journalistic pieces. Having evaded death at Auschwitz, Borowski committed suicide by turning on the gas in his Warsaw apartment in 1951 at the age of 28.

These brief summaries cannot, of course, do justice to the subtleties of Miłosz's portraits in *The Captive Mind.* I have distilled from them only the judgements which Miłosz makes about each of these writers as he describes their literary careers, their work, and the political and ideological meanderings which eventually led to their alliance with Communist power. Miłosz is not uncharitable in his portraits, but he is, like the Communist ideologues whom he opposes, dogmatic in his pronouncements. He allows no other possible interpretations to enter into play. The reader who does not know Polish literature, who cannot decipher the Greek code letters attached to these writers, is swept along by the force of the argument. One who knows something of what Miłosz is describing may disagree, perhaps, over certain details of interpretation, but that is really not the point. *The Captive Mind* is not an exercise in literary criticism; for that one should read Miłosz's *The History of Polish Literature,* written some fifteen years later, in which the four writers receive somewhat different treatment from that given them in *The Captive Mind.*[13] Nor is *The Captive Mind* a collection of documented intellectual biographies. Rather, it is an impassioned warning about the dangers lying in wait for those who would attempt to come to grips with the infernal question of how the individual can maintain his moral integrity while engaging, of necessity, in the historical situation into which he has been thrust by chance.

The Captive Mind has the form of a naturalist's guide to the exotic species of the East European intellectual in the first post-war decade. It has the force of an Old Testament jeremiad in which the author renders a fierce moral judgement against those who will not recognise that to play the game of "ketman" is to barter one's soul. Miłosz insists that men must recognise moral absolutes, and take their stand in defence of what is right:

> To demand that a man regard the present as he would the past without, as my friend said, worrying about trifles, that he gaze at the ripening fruits of tomorrow through the telescope of History—that is asking too much. There must be, after all, some standard one dare not destroy lest the fruits of tomorrow prove to be rotten. If I think thus it is because for

> the last two thousand years or more there have been not only brigands, conquistadors, and hangmen, but also people for whom evil was evil and had to be called evil.[14]

Lurking behind the four biographies of *The Captive Mind* is another life story—that of Miłosz himself, in whom, one senses, these four lives elicited the tremulous feeling, "There but for the grace of God. . . ." That life story, presented in far greater detail and in a leisurely chronological manner, with emphasis on the cultural milieu in which Miłosz lived, was finally written down in *Native Realm.* A former colleague of mine once told me that as a poet himself he had found Miłosz's autobiography curiously unsatisfying. He had wanted to find out what were the motive forces inside this man whose translated poetry he had read with reverence. And he had, to his great disappointment, discovered very little of what he sought. He had expected intimate revelations of emotional traumas, of psychological twists, and what he had found instead were ruminations on Catholicism, Polishness, and Marxism as a historical mix at a certain point in the continuum of human existence. As the subtitle of the English version specifies, *Native Realm* is a *A Search for Self-Definition,* an exploration of the formative moral, intellectual and historical experiences which led Miłosz to act as he did, to judge as he does. It is an extremely powerful work, which derives its force not from the sometimes didactic moralising of *The Captive Mind* but from Miłosz's extraordinary ability to make the clash of ideas and ethics come alive in all its intellectual and emotional potency.

Native Realm leads us through Miłosz's life from childhood through the decision to emigrate to the West, and ends with a two-part essay on "Tiger," written in the style of the sketches in *The Captive Mind.* It is fitting that Miłosz should have concluded his autobiography with the story of another man's fate, for Miłosz sees his own life as a set of choices from a finite number of options—those options being determined by his historical and cultural milieu. Only by analysing the milieu and observing the configurations of other men's choices within it can one begin to comprehend the life which is the subject of an autobiography. Miłosz describes this approach to autobiography as a method which "look[s] upon oneself as a sociological phenomenon."[15]

It will not have escaped the reader's attention that in reviewing the four character sketches in *The Captive Mind* I neglected to identify "Alpha." I should like to turn to his story now. As Miłosz presents him, "Alpha" (his good friend, the novelist Jerzy Andrzejewski) had a strong need to be recognised as a person of great moral authority. Before the War, Andrzejewski was famous as a Catholic novelist; during the Occupation he was known for his stories about moral choice under duress, about loyalty in the face of despair. He was eventually to become a Communist writer, then to be among the first in 1955/56 to criticise the Communist system of thought control. At the time we are speaking of, Andrzejewski had recently published his famous novel, *Popiół i diament* (which was later published in English in 1962 as *Ashes and Diamonds*), now known world-wide through its numerous translated versions and from the superb film made from the novel by the Polish director, Andrzej Wajda.[16]

The popularity of *Ashes and Diamonds* is easy to account for. It is a well-made novel, neatly constructed, simple to follow, plausible, and intensely engaging. Its action unfolds during the four days preceding the German surrender on May 8, 1945. Andrzejewski's aim is to reveal the social disorder in Poland as the country embarks on its transition from the dislocations of war to the task of building a new society under Communist guidance. Set in a provincial town already occupied (or "liberated") by the Red Army, the novel offers us an array of characters who represent the various social, political, and generational strata of urban Polish society at war's end. One of the two leading characters, and the novel's moral centre, is Szczuka, an old Communist recently returned from a German concentration camp. He is on assignment to mobilise Communist adherents among the working class. Szczuka is portrayed as a man who has suffered much for his beliefs, who is clearly aware that the masses of Polish workers do not support the Communists, and who is nonetheless unswervingly dedicated to the cause of establishing Communist power in Poland as a prelude to building a just society.

Maciej Chełmicki is the other leading protagonist. He is a young man in his early twenties, a survivor of the Warsaw Uprising. Chełmicki, whom History has turned into a trained killer, is under assignment by the Home Army (the major underground partisan force during the Occupation, which owed its allegiance to the London-based government-in-exile). His task is to kill Szczuka. The first political event of the novel is a failed assassination attempt in which two workers are killed instead of Szczuka. The novel ends with Chełmicki shooting Szczuka and then being gunned down himself by an army patrol. Between the two events Chełmicki discovers for the first time in his violent life the tenderness of love. The assassination is carried out as his last act of loyalty to the partisans after which he intends to build a new life as a civilian. Szczuka's death is a terrible loss because he is one of the few humane Communists portrayed in this book. Maciej Chełmicki's death is pointless. The final grief-stricken words of the novel belong to the soldier who shot Chełmicki and who, finding no gun on the dying man, assumes he has shot an innocent person. The soldier cries out, "Why were you running, brother?"

The note of pity on which *Ashes and Diamonds* ends is heard throughout the novel. Chełmicki and the anonymous soldier are not the only ones who have been made into murderers by force of historical circumstance and against their better natures. A subplot involves a group of teenagers, raised since childhood in an atmosphere of violence and conspiracy, who commit murder and lesser crimes as they bend together, jockeying for power and prestige in imitation of the underground conspiracies of their elders.

Although Andrzejewski shows a great deal of compassion for the youth whose lives have been so distorted and who have simply had precious little opportunity to evolve a moral system of their own, his attitude towards their elders is generally contemptuous. Another subplot of *Ashes and Diamonds* involves a group of aristocrats who are planning their escape from Poland. These people are allowed no redeeming features, and the last scene in which we see them—a grotesque evocation of the dance at the end of Stanisław Wyspiański's play, *Wesele* (The Wedding) (1901)—has them drunkenly dancing the Polonaise at the dawn of freedom with a motley crew of entertainers, lawyers, and others drawn from the ranks of the demoralised bourgeoisie.[17]

Andrzejewski was not so simplistic as to argue that all right is on the side of the Communists, all wrong amongst those who are in opposition. He introduces a number of characters who are Communists out of mere opportunism, and a colonel of the Home Army who, though he is upholding what for Andrzejewski was a wrong and lost cause, at least possesses dignity, courage, and the strength of a firm conviction. In his discussion of *Ashes and Diamonds* and *The Captive Mind*, Miłosz convincingly suggests that the great virtue of Andrzejewski's novel is pity, but that its dominant emotion is "a feeling of anger *against the losers.*"[18]

In comparison with Soviet Russian books about the building of Communist society, *Ashes and Diamonds* appears almost miraculous. The reader is struck by Andrzejewski's compassion, by his willingness to admit that not all Communist Party members are as sage as Szczuka, that not all opponents of the regime are as rabid as the character, Count Puciatycki. But there is a hollow core in *Ashes and Diamonds*, a great emptiness left there by things unsaid, issues ignored. Miłosz attributes this to a moral flaw in

Andrzejewski's personality, and implicitly discounts the probable ravages of censorship. It is impossible to determine from the published text how genuine was Andrzejewski's infatuation with the Communist future, how much of his work was the product of revulsion against the past, how much a laudable effort to plead for compassion for the Home Army partisans cooped up in Polish jails at the time *Ashes and Diamonds* was written.

The central missing ingredient in *Ashes and Diamonds* is a recognition of what Communism was really like in the Soviet Union. Only for a moment is this issue broached, in the hesitant questioning of Szczuka's old friend, the venerable socialist leader, Kalicki, now clearly consigned to the dust bin of History. But Kalicki does not address the issues that any real socialist would have raised: the perversion of the dictatorship of the proletariat into a police state, the purges, and the millions of prisoners in the vast network of the Soviet concentration camp system, all of which was witnessed and suffered by the Poles who had fled to the East in 1939. And by limiting his Communist characters to those who had spent the War years either in German concentration camps or in the parts of Poland not occupied by the Red Army, Andrzejewski avoided having to deal with the knowledge about Soviet power that Polish returnees, former prisoners almost to a man, would have brought back with them.

Another obvious gap in *Ashes and Diamonds* which, like the silence about the Soviet system, becomes especially obvious when the novel is compared with *The Seizure of Power*, is the utter lack of references to the exterminated Polish Jews or to the Jewish survivors.

Concluding his discussion of Andrzejewski in *The Captive Mind*, Miłosz attempted to pin down the essential differences between himself and Andrzejewski that had led these two friends, both writers with a highly developed social conscience and a sense of moral duty, to choose such different political paths. Miłosz writes:

> It is not my place to judge. I myself traveled the same road of seeming inevitability. In fleeing I trampled on many virtues that may determine the worth of a man. So I judge myself severely though my sins are not the same as his. Perhaps the difference in our destinies lay in a minute disparity in our reactions when we visited the ruins of Warsaw or gazed out the window at the [Home Army] prisoners. I felt that I could not write of these things unless I wrote the *whole* truth, not just a part.[19]

It is not implausible, I think, especially in the light of Miłosz's intense preoccupation with the morality of Andrzejewski's literary practice, to read

The Seizure of Power as a response to *Ashes and Diamonds.* I want to make it clear that I am not calling Miłosz's novel a simple rebuttal of Andrzejewski's book. Miłosz does not come out in support of the socialists, most of whom, indeed, he shows as politically inept or outmoded at best. Nor does he demonstrate any yearning for a return to the old ruling class; he does not even bother to caricature them, so insignificant a factor are they in his conception of the struggle for political realignment which is the subject of *The Seizure of Power.* References to old guard emigrés by the characters closest to Miłosz ideologically make this contempt explicit.

Miłosz's novel is an attempt to tell "the *whole* truth" by confronting the complex issue of how the educated stratum of an exhausted nation, including both Poles and Jews, schooled in the realities of brute power, came to terms with the historical position in which Poland found itself from approximately 1945 through 1951. The vexing issue of a choice to be made not between two clearly opposed alternatives of good and bad, historically valid and historically doomed, as Andrzejewski would have us believe, but among possibilities every one of which was tainted or foul, is the central concern of Miłosz's book. In *The Seizure of Power* Miłosz dramatises through fictional means what in *The Captive Mind* and *Native Realm* he demonstrated through intellectual analysis: the broad spectrum of motivations and hesitancies among those who wished to find a way to shape Poland's political development and to make for themselves a bearable life, preferably without risk of imprisonment.

The cast of characters in *The Seizure of Power* is fairly large. The "action" is basically cerebral: the characters seek answers to the question of how to behave politically. The most important characters are Professor Gil, a classical Greek scholar, engaged in a translation of Thucydides' *History of the Peloponnesian Wars* in lieu of teaching at the university from which he had been fired as an outmoded bourgeois intellectual, and Piotr Kwinto, a young writer and student of French literature, who has returned to Poland as an officer in the Red Army. Kwinto and Gil give us complementary chronological perspectives on the events in Poland. Gil and his daughter, Joanna, transport us back in time to the disaster of the Warsaw Uprising—the utter waste of lives caused jointly by Nazi viciousness, intransigent Polish romantic nationalism, and the cynical Soviet decision to withhold Red Army support so that the troublesome Warsaw underground could be destroyed by the Germans. The portrayal of the decimation of Warsaw is part if the indictment against the Communists, who eagerly arrest and execute young Home Army soldiers inspired by simple patriotism, while recruiting as collaborators such fascist ideologues as Michał Kamieński (a fictional counterpart of the real Bolesław Piasecki). In Gil's thoughts about his neighbour, the janitor's daughter who has been granted access to education but not to knowledge, we catch some glimpses of the new proletarian society in the making. And it is Gil, reading the daily newspapers, who informs us of the show trials and purges by which the seizure of power is consolidated. While Gil shows us the outer chronological boundaries of the action, Kwinto conducts us through the time between these points when choices could still be made, however painfully.

It is tempting to view Gil and Kwinto as encompassing two aspects of Miłosz's personality. Gil is given to meditation on the vagaries of history; as a translator he is concerned with using words as precisely and accurately as possible. He is a moralist with a firm sense of right and wrong. Through his work on Thucydides, Gil provides the long historical view in which the Communist takeover of Poland must be seen, confirming that war and vicious factional strife are an old occurrence in human history. Gil's meditations on such themes inform us, as does Miłosz's decisive declaration in *The Captive Mind* about the moral necessity of calling evil evil, that there are moral absolutes to which one must adhere. They also conform to Tiger's belief: ". . . woe to those who think that in the twentieth century they can save themselves without taking part in the tragedy, without purifying themselves through historical suffering."[20]

Piotr Kwinto worries about his social responsibilities; he has no love for the class injustices of the old regime, and he knows only too well the viciousness of life in the Soviet Union where he has been a prisoner. As a student of poetry Kwinto worries that literature may be a luxury and a form of self-indulgence in hard political times. Kwinto wants to be useful to his country; he also wants to make a reasonably good life for himself. Eventually he offers his services to the Party and is named a foreign correspondent. His assignment abroad thus allies him with the Party while at the same time it places him in a position from which he can defect should he decide to do so. In fact, the reader knows, although Kwinto does not, that the plane that carries him abroad has taken off only moments before the security police arrive at the airfield to arrest him. This is the last we see of Kwinto; we are not told what happens to him on foreign soil.

Through Kwinto and his associates we see the agony of choosing sides in history. Kwinto has connections with a number of significant characters. These include Winter, a Jewish Communist, whose parents were killed by the Nazis, whose child died in Soviet Central Asia, whose guilty conscience upbraids him for having denounced his friend Kwinto and caused his arrest out of a cowardly fear of being arrested himself, who sticks with the Communists and their deterministic ideology out of a metaphysical fear of a world devoid of meaning. Winter, who ultimately accepts a diplomatic post in the Party's service, is described at one point in the novel as experiencing the torment of those who have once been converted to a belief in Marxism-Leninism and can never again live with it.

> . . . what would be left for him if he betrayed the Party? Where could he find meaning if by his decision he attempted to prove that history has no meaning? He envied his uncle and people like him because they had never known that moment of poisonous enlightenment which is like the taste of the apple ripped from the tree of knowledge.[21]

Winter's yearning to believe in historical meaning, however repellent it may be, is, of course, consonant with the major themes of both *The Captive Mind* and *Native Realm*.

In addition to Winter, we meet through Kwinto two other Jewish intellectuals. One is Julian Halpern, who has joined the Communists out of hatred for the nationalist underground organizations which would not take him in after his escape from the Warsaw Ghetto. The other is Bruno, an assimilated Jewish writer who survived by masquerading as an "Aryan," and who is wracked by guilt because he does not write on Jewish themes and uses Polish, not Yiddish, to express himself. Bruno's grief over the fate of the Polish Jews leads Kwinto to contemplate his own sense of guilt at having been merely a person of good will who did nothing positive to stem the swelling tide of anti-Semitism in the years before the War.

At every turn in this novel we are confronted with the impossibility of finding a course of action in history which would be completely consonant with moral precepts, which would involve no degrading compromises. No one in the novel achieves such moral purity for it is clearly unattainable, but lines are drawn between those who make a valiant effort in this difficult spiritual enterprise, and those who do not recognise the demands of conscience.

It must be said that as a work of fiction, rather than as a dramatised moral/political treatise, *The Seizure of Power* leaves something to be desired. In this hastily written novel Miłosz chose to use a cinematic technique which moves in short scenes from character to character, and includes a number of flashbacks and cuts from one location to another. This technique had the virtue of allowing him to include a fairly large number of participants, many of whom are just episodic characters. Its chronological and spatial fluidity gave him the freedom to touch upon a broad range of topics and events, from the Warsaw Uprising through the creeping imposition of Stalinism to the purge trials which ended the transition period; from the question of Polish nationalism to the evaluation of historical materialism; from the question of Jewish existence in a Polish state to the issue of Polish existence in the Soviet Russian empire.

The most obvious negative aspect of such an approach is that it leaves room for only superficial treatment of each of its many subjects in the course of what is only a very slim book. The novel is often at risk of turning into a compendium of shorthand allusions to all the political and social problems besetting Poland in the early post-War years.

Another drawback of this approach is its unsuitability for sustained character development. As we watch the major characters struggle morally and intellectually with their political identities, we cannot always perceive them as real individuals rather than incarnate political positions. We know too little about their personalities, the shaping forces other than historical circumstance which have made them what they are. Consequently, there is an odour of caricature or type-casting about them. Professor Gil, for example, is the quiet introspective scholar, saved by his deep knowledge of the classics. But as Miłosz knows, and showed so powerfully in *Native Realm, The Captive Mind,* "Traktat moralny" ("Moral Treatise,") and elsewhere, people are not always whole: there are those who can read Thucydides at home and yet play a vicious public role. Why, one wonders, is Professor Gil, who appears to be the somewhat compromised ethical pillar of the book, the man that he is? And what made Winter become a Communist originally? Was it his Jewish otherness and lack of faith in a controlling divinity? These are the kinds of biographical questions that Miłosz attempted to come to grips with in the nonfictional prose treatments of the subject. Such questions are not dealt with in *The Seizure of Power*—to its detriment.

Only in the case of Piotr Kwinto does Miłosz attempt to give a psychological explanation, but in this instance the result is quite clumsy. Kwinto has a dream in which Stalin appears as the dispenser of all nourishment, the source of all protection. The victim's attraction to the wielder of total power is an important psychological issue, and well worth exploring. But the psychological explanation offered by Miłosz is simplistic. It is that because Kwinto's father died in the 1920–21 war between Poland and the Soviet

Union, when the boy was only six years old, the orphaned Kwinto has been seeking a father all his life and finds him in the omnipotent figure of Joseph Stalin. This interpretation simply does not correspond to all the other information about Kwinto scattered throughout the novel. In fact, it is countered by the cynical remarks about Kwinto made earlier in the novel by the chief of Party propaganda, Baruga (a fictional representation of Jerzy Borejsza). Baruga's crude psychologising avoids personal explanations and points directly and gleefully to the warping experience of life in a Soviet labour camp:

> He had been too badly bruised for it not to have left some definite traces. Whoever once tastes that bitterness walks around as if nothing's wrong, but everything's been turned upside down within him. Give him ruins, terror, poverty, and he'll yearn for gardens, cottages with green blinds, and peace. But drop him into the midst of *Gemütlichkeit* and he'll howl and writhe. He's missing the tiny part that once made it possible for him to tolerate all of that. And the meaninglessness of life will choke him. That's when we get them. When they feel the meaninglessness of life they're ours. Then they want to act, to act at any price. And who if not we can give them the moment of delight, the intoxicating sense that they are demigods?[22]

This interpretation, too, does not quite seem to fit the character of Piotr Kwinto, although it is extremely revealing of Baruga.

The groping and fumbling of the characters in *The Seizure of Power*, however realistic this may be as a portrayal of process, threatens the fictional work with disintegration. I believe that this is the novel's ethical virtue, and also its most serious aesthetic flaw. Such explosive and untidy material seems to demand a looser and probably larger novelistic form. Only simplification in the manner of *Ashes and Diamonds* lends itself to the form of the short realistic novel. Miłosz, by attempting to contain his material in a short representational form, was driven to use a number of awkward devices in order to maintain control. The first of these, the exclusion of more than a bare minimum of relevant background material for the characters, is linked to a lack of authorial analysis. More obtrusive than this is the overuse of coincidence and crossed plot lines to unify the kaleidoscopic movement of the novel. Ultimately, almost all the characters' lives cross—if not directly then through an intermediary. The coincidences involved in producing such a neat structure strain credulity and undermine the intellectual credibility of this novel which otherwise aims at a level-headed and realistic portrayal of a politically chaotic time.

Miłosz's message to the West demanded lucid analysis and a prophetic voice, and for this the straightforward genre of the essay, with its unabashed display of critical intelligence applied *ex post facto* to events, is perhaps best suited. *The Captive Mind* and *Native Realm,* each incorporating aspects of the analytical essay and setting them within a context of moral passion, engage the reader's attention both by force of intellectual persuasion and by demonstration of the spiritual urgency of the issues described. *The Seizure of Power,* though it uses precisely the same political material, is pallid and even flaccid by contrast, and does not persuade the reader of the urgent reality of its fictionalised problems. The positive characters in the novel are all still trying to comprehend fully the situation they are in; only the dogmatists, the fanatic nationalists or such representatives of Communist power as security chief Wolin and propaganda chief Baruga, have the certainty which Miłosz, the essayist who *has made his choice,* displays in *The Captive Mind* and *Native Realm.*

In underlining the common concerns in Milosz's political prose of the 1950s I have, of necessity, paid scant attention to the differences among these works and, especially, to the nonpolitical aspects of *Native Realm* which distinguish it from the other two. Before concluding my discussion of *The Captive Mind, The Seizure of Power,* and *Native Realm,* however, I should like to point out that there is a subtle shift in emphasis between the first two works, which preceded the thawing of Stalinism in Eastern Europe, and *Native Realm,* which was written after the Thaw. The main goal of *The Captive Mind* and *The Seizure of Power* was to alert the West to the dangers of flirting with a dialectical defence of historical determinism, and to issue an urgent warning about the determined thrust of Soviet imperialism. The East European intellectuals in these works are cautionary figures in an on-going morality play whose action is the struggle for men's minds and souls.

In *Native Realm,* however, which I believe is close to the evaluation of these events now held by Miłosz, the East European intellectual is shown to be, by virtue of his more sinister experience, one step ahead of his Western counterparts in the sphere of moral maturity. The awful burden of choice, which was dramatised in *The Seizure of Power* but not shown in that bleak novel to have any conceivable positive value, becomes at the close of *Native Realm* the first stage towards a true moral understanding. By a dialectical inversion, what was earlier presented as a totally negative experience is later shown to bear the seeds of a sombre wisdom. In his autobiography, Miłosz's political warning to the West to shun the dangers of Communism shades into an admonition to learn from the Eastern experience the values of humility, self-doubt, and Christian love. Since the search for religious understanding and faith has been such an important concern of Miłosz ever since he, in effect, exorcised his political demons by the writing of the prose works we have been considering here, it may be appropriate to close this discussion with the final paragraphs of *Native Realm*, which serve as a summation of Miłosz's political experience and a transition to the more philosophical concerns of the works of the last two decades:

> We Easterners . . . precisely because we had to gaze into the hells of our century, made the discovery that the elixir of youth is not a delusion. . . . No one brought himself willingly to look into those hells. Time that was compressed, speeded up, was not physiological time; it, too, avenged itself with a concentration camp, a bullet, or a heart attack. Nevertheless, it taught us the meaning of full commitment and exploded the barriers between the individual and the social, between style and institution, between aesthetics and politics. That miraculous elixir is nothing other than the certainty that there are no boundaries to the knowledge of what is human; that to puff ourselves up with self-importance is inappropriate because each of our achievements falls into yesterday. . . .
>
> Through defeats and disasters, humanity searches for the elixir of youth: that is, of life made into thought, that ardor that upholds belief in the wider usefulness of our individual effort, even if it apparently changes nothing in the iron working of the world. It may be that we Easterners have been given the lead in this search. By choosing, we had to give up some values for the sake of others, which is the essence of tragedy. Yet only such an experience can whet our understanding, so that we see an old truth in a new light: when ambition counsels us to lift ourselves above simple moral rules guarded by the poor in spirit, rather than to choose them as our compass needle amid the uncertainties of change, we stifle the only thing that can redeem our follies and our mistakes: love.[23]

Notes

1. The prose of Cz. Miłosz was recently analysed by Wł. Bolecki but he passes over in silence the aspect under discussion in this article. See Wł. Bolecki, "Proza Miłosza," *Pamiętnik Literacki* 75, part 2 (1984), pp. 133–64. Bolecki concentrates on two novels only: *The Seizure of Power* and *The Issa Valley*.
2. Cz. Miłosz, *The Land of Ulro* (New York: Farrar Straus Giroux, 1984), p. 4. For the original see Cz. Miłosz, *Ziemia Ulro* (Paris: Instytut Literacki, 1977), p. 20.
3. Miłosz, *The Land of Ulro*, p. 23; for the original see Miłosz, *Ziemia Ulro*, p. 33.
4. Cz. Miłosz, *La prise du pouvoir* (Paris: Gaillimard, 1953); Cz. Miłosz, *Zdobycie władzy* (Paris: Instytut Literacki, 1953); Cz. Miłosz, *The Seizure of Power*, translated by Celina Wieniawska (New York: Criterion, 1955).
5. Cz. Miłosz, *Zniewolony umysł* (Paris: Instytut Literacki, 1953); Cz. Miłosz, *The Captive Mind*, translated by Jane Zielonko (New York: Knopf, 1953).
6. Cz. Miłosz, *Rodzinna Europa* (Paris: Instytut Literacki, 1959); Cz. Miłosz, *Native Realm: A Search for Self-Definition*, translated by Catherine S. Leach (New York: Doubleday, 1968).
7. Miłosz, *Native Realm*, p. 2.
8. Miłosz, *The Captive Mind*, p. 207.
9. Miłosz, *Native Realm*, p. 268.
10. Ibid., p. 286. Tiger refers to the Polish philosopher Tadeusz Kroński.
11. Ibid., p. 297.
12. For the original see Miłosz, *Zdobycie władzy*, pp. 90–92. Translation by M. Levine.
13. Cz. Miłosz, *The History of Polish Literature* (New York: Macmillan, 1969). Compare pp. 409–11, 413, 488–93.
14. Miłosz, *The Captive Mind*, pp. 214–15.
15. Miłosz, *Native Realm*, p. 5.
16. J. Andrzejewski, *Popiół i diament* (Warsaw: Czytelnik, 1948); J. Andrzejewski, *Ashes and Diamonds*, translated by David Welsh (London: Weidenfeld & Nicolson, 1962).
17. Sł. Mrożek, in his article "Popiół? Diament?" *Kultura*, no. 1–2 (1983), pp. 31–41, directed a strong attack against J. Andrzejewski's novel, suggesting that the author harboured in it an intolerable falsification of Polish reality immediately after the war.
18. Miłosz, *The Captive Mind*, p. 100.
19. Ibid., 104.
20. Miłosz, *Native Realm*, p. 267.
21. For the original see Miłosz, *Zdobycie władzy*, p. 124. Translation by M. Levine.
22. Ibid., p. 110.
23. Miłosz, *Native Realm*, p. 300.

PAUL COATES

Irony and Choice

Miłosz in the Late Forties and Early Fifties

Agnostic Dialectics

For Miłosz, the progression of events is an inscrutable phantasmagoria. "Równina" ("A Plain"), from the wartime volume *Ocalenie* (Rescue), ends with the image of the rainbow rising:

> Z nieznanej ziemi w nieznane niebiosa.
>
> ("Równina," *O*)

> From the unknown earth to the unknown skies.
>
> ("A Plain," tr. P.C.)

The agnostic gesture is repeated at the end of "Zmieniał się język" ("The Language Changed"):

> Ani takie to było jak raz się wydało,
> Ani takie jak teraz układasz w opowieść.
>
> (Zmieniał się język," *GZ*, 13)

Neither it was as it appeared to be
Nor as later you put into a tale.
("The Language Changed," tr. E.M.)

Everything is transient: in terms of "Równina" again:

Twierdze czerwone, rozchwiane stolice.
Skrzydeł na niebie i drutów potoki
Na chwilę są i sypią się w pył.
("Równina," *O*)

Red fortresses, hazy big cities,
Streams of wings and wires in the sky
Exist for a moment and disintegrate.
("A Plain," tr. E.M.)

Because all things are ephemeral, the objects singled out for mention in "Równina" have an accidental air, as if they have been chosen arbitrarily by a verse that identifies with history's movement towards the great blankness of the unknown, which is also the wide expanse of the plain. The arbitrariness with which the objects mentioned are selected is part of Miłosz's classicism: incidents and things illustrate theses rather than radiating the glow of the Romantic symbol. Miłosz's sceptical sense of the relativity of the momentary would-be absolute orders established by history renders it difficult for him to formulate reasons for the rejection or acceptance of any particular order. Whence the lengthy period of meditation required before he was able to decide to reject the postwar, *soi-disant* socialist order established in Poland. Indeed, at first he seems to have sympathized with some of its features. The prewar intellectual, indifferent to private property, felt probably a certain *Schadenfreude* when the small shops were closed and the petty bourgeois entrepreneurial spirit doused. Nevertheless, the "dialectical flexibility" Miłosz ascribes to himself in *Rodzinna Europa (Native Realm)* as the characteristic trait of the scion of a ruined household—a flexibility which leads the masters of dialectic who seize power in 1944 to see in him a possible political ally—is finally so flexible as to turn against the dialecticians themselves. Thus in Miłosz one has the paradox of the dialectician driven by the contradictions of the dialectic to *assert* the values of common sense: the prescription of "Rosół, befsztyk, mleko" (*SD*) ["Broth, steak, milk"], extolled in "Traktat Moralny" ("Moral Treatise").

Miłosz/Brecht/Conrad

Although Miłosz and Brecht have very little in common with one another, it is worthwhile for a moment noting the similarity in the way in which they employ dialectic in order to arrive at an advocacy of "das plumpe Denken" (Brecht's version of beefsteak and milk). There is even a similarity in the course of their poetic development, from an overwrought and apocalyptic style to a more casual and intimate one that distrusts the grandiloquence of prophecy. It was this achieved asceticism which gave the two poets their exemplary authority after the war: their sobriety had the chastened tone of the survivor. When World War Two tested the private apocalypse of Miłosz's catastrophism against reality, it tempered his style to its true tone: the survivor's philosophical wonder at the fact that things still exist at all. If Miłosz's poetry is generally less successful in achieving impersonality than Brecht's, it may be because it lacks the dramatist's faculty of self-projection into a mask or a persona. It may also be that detachment came easier to the older, worldlier poet. The facial contortions and shifts of stylistic register induced by conflicting emotions are clearly visible in Miłosz's work during this period, whilst in Brecht's they are concealed by the mask of the canny peasant. They dictate the desperate, final couplet of the famous "Który skrzywdziłeś" ("You Who Wronged") and the uneasy ditherings of "Traktat Moralny" (a poem I will return to later). The stem from the self's propensity "do spożywania rzeczy niesmacznych, właśnie dlatego że są niesmaczne" (*RE*, 96) ["... for swallowing unpleasant things just because they are unpleasant" (*NR*, 113)]: a perverse inclination well-attuned to the contortions of the dialectician denounced in much of Miłosz's other work. The mind's distaste for the things it tastes persuades it to abstract itself from all events, to view history as a meaningless parade of occurrence. Here Miłosz's position is closer to that of Conrad than that of Brecht. It is surely significant that both men should have been self-exiled from their countries: the illusoriness of the events that occur in one's new homeland, their failure to engage one, combines with one's fading memory of one's old country to reinforce the view that all things are an illusion; whilst at the same time each man's fear of the consequences of his own nihilism impels him to attach himself with desperate tenacity to something that will outlast the corrosions of time. For Conrad, it is human fidelity: for Miłosz, the attachment to Christian tradition. This is not to say, however, that Miłosz is a Christian poet, even though he often talks of demons. Rather, he is a Christian *fellow traveller* (akin in some ways to his near-contemporary Auden).

The Involution of Irony

The above can be seen as a prologue to the theme of this paper: the nature of the irony of Miłosz. It can be seen to operate at three levels at least: against those who were contented with prewar order in Poland, with all its injustices; against the postwar dialecticians who proclaim the surmounting of the old contradictions and injustices whilst themselves establishing new ones; and, finally, and most problematically, against the self that gains from its own masochistic propensity to taste the distasteful, a troubling insight into the masochism with which Polish communists concede to the *force majeure* of the logic of a history that promotes *Russian* interests. This is the source of the strange and disturbing double focus of *Zniewolony umysł (The Captive Mind),* which preserves it from the naïve self-righteousness of the cold warriors who have so often, and so mistakenly, adopted Miłosz. It is the dual focus of a man who anatomises in others a temptation he himself feels to be a very real one; and whose ferocity of inquisition is tempered by knowledge of his own fallibility, which leads him to speak of "Alpha" and "Beta" rather than "Andrzejewski" or "Borowski." The allegorical veiling admits that the accounts Miłosz has to settle are "prywatne obowiązki" [personal business]: he will not wash his fellow-victims' dirty linen in public. Or rather—and this is why his position is so ambiguous—he will do his washing out in the open, but behind a semi-transparent veil. A latter-day Dante, Miłosz places his acquaintances in Hell. The apocalyptic vision of communism serves the same function as Miłosz's catastrophist visions of the thirties: it asserts pride and superiority. All other arguments than one's own will soon be swept away. And yet Miłosz is aware of the anachronism of the Dantesque position in the present day (even though it is one often adopted by modern Poles). It is not done to place one's contemporaries in Hell any longer. And so one masks one's biographies by using initials. This may be intended to demonstrate the *typical,* supra-personal nature of the problems exemplified by the lives one is considering, but it also protects the author in two ways: firstly, by warding off the accusation of personal malice; and, secondly, by throwing the reader onto the defence by withholding certain information, arousing both his talent for allegory (and for self-congratulation, and hence acceptance of the allegorical text, once he has deciphered it) and his anxiety. In the final reckoning, Miłosz's professions of personal fallibility can seem to protest too much, and to be merely tactical.

Miłosz's irony is an anguished one. Its torment is due to the self's inability to extricate itself from history and its contradictions. In *Rodzinna Europa* he describes himself as apparently a Polish State cultural attaché, and yet actually surrounded by the ghosts of the Polish past; these ghosts are invisible to the Washington milieux that deem him merely a representative of a red government; and their invisibility mortifies him, for it prevents others perceiving that he is not what he seems to be. Exhibitionistic display of the contradictions of the self thus becomes a form of pride and self-definition: it demonstrates one's complexity as a higher being. This proud, anguished irony is the dominant feature of *Światło dzienne* (Daily Light), the fruit of a period in which Miłosz attempted the self-definition that is the necessary prelude to an irrevocable choice. The very first poem in the collection announces that its patron will be Swift— the practitioner of an irony that finally resisted its master. The same will be true of Miłosz, since the sheer diversity of kinds of poems included in the volume indicates an uneven development of the self, a conflict of unmastered emotions.

Perhaps the most successfully ironic poem in *Światło dzienne* is "Dziecię Europy" ("Child of Europe"), an impassioned denunciation by mimicry of the masters of double-think, the cynics who are ever ready to discard friends, town and country ("Nie kochaj żadnego kraju . . . Nie kochaj żadnego miasta . . . Nie miej czułości dla ludzi," (*SD*) ["Love no country . . . Love no city . . . Do not love people" (*SP*, 63)], the poet ironically advises the child of Europe) in order to survive. The poem's sheer repetitiveness is very impressive; it is achieved through the self's mocking adoption of the voice of the cynics, who are thus seen to condemn themselves out of their own mouths: a self-projection by Miłosz that is the exception to the rule of his work I mentioned earlier when contrasting him with Brecht. "Dziecię Europy" is a powerful dramatic monologue. But its very impressiveness is the fruit of a significant omission—that of the poet himself, the first person. The poem eloquently tells us what the poet opposes. Its sheer consistency prompts one to wonder what the poet himself approves of. Miłosz himself seems to have wondered too, for later in the volume he attempts in "Traktat moralny" to give sage recommendations. "Traktat moralny" thus complements "Dziecię Europy": the first person omitted from the latter expatiates at length in the former. Its attempt to formulate positive recommendations proves misconceived however. Towards the end of the poem its speaker concedes "nie mam ja recepty" (*SD*) ["I do not have the recipe" (tr. E.M.)] having already trivialized his own experience by filtering it through unconvincing allusions. To drink vodka is to resemble the Brothers Karamazov; to read Sartre is to be like the devil—séparé de lui-même. The poem is trivial in the manner of Auden's verse letters: the silliness of the final reference to "Heart of Darkness" undercuts its intended ominousness. It has the embarrassed air of a man asked for advice who has no advice to give but seeks to bluster his way through his discomfiture. It is shot through with the dyspeptic bewilderment of someone who senses that something ominous is occurring (a dissociation of sensibility, as it were), but does not know how to combat it and fritters away his time in literary charades. Irony gives way to shrugs of the shoulder.

The Uneven Development of the Self

The various incompatible poetic notes struck in *Światło dzienne* indicate the "niejednolitość" [disproportionality] Miłosz discerns and laments in himself in *Rodzinna Europa*. The unevenness is linked, I think, to the fundamental theme of Miłosz's work, which is transience. It is the theme of "Traktat poetycki" ("Poetic Treatise") or "Zmieniał się język" which are cast in the mode of musing recollection attended by philosophical wonder both over the fact of one's present existence—one could so easily have died—and the existence of anything at all, and are among his best works. The link between irony, transience and the variability of tone is found in the statement by Goethe's Mephistopheles that "alles, was entsteht / Ist wert, dass es zugrunde geht." It is echoed by Miłosz himself when he says that a particular order "jest, jak każdy ład, dojrzały do klęski" (*RE*, 217) ["... is, like every order, ripe for destruction" (*NR*, 262)]. Because nothing lasts, because the apocalypse will soon sweep all things into oblivion, writing is a sheer luxury. The impending catastrophe will destroy the possible audience— Miłosz does not hide his wonder over the fact that the world still exists at all—and no monuments will outlive the present age. Miłosz's work had been widely praised by those, such as Donald Davie, whose ideal of the poet is that of a man speaking to other men. Miłosz's sense of his own complex singularity combines with his real exile to make him doubt the possibility of any such direct address. He gently mocks his own classical nostalgia for convention (the stiltedness of those conventions reveals itself in his "Do Tadeusza Różewicza, poety" ("To the Poet Tadeusz Różewicz"), conscious of the incompatibility of convention with the uneven self. For modern culture fails to impose a single form on its inhabitants, and thus on its poets. The problem of form prompts one to compare Miłosz to Gombrowicz: unlike in so many respects, they resemble each other in their "niejednolitość" (and in linking "dojrzałość" with destruction, as in the quotation from *Rodzinna Europa (Native Realm)* given above). For Miłosz, it is the sheer diversity of the cultures he has experienced that precludes unification of the self; for Gombrowicz, it is the persistence within a single person of the hardened, incompatible attitudes of different stages of one's life. If Miłosz's work is less impressive than that of Gombrowicz—particularly the latter's first three works, *Bakakaj* (Bakakai), *Ferdydurke* and *Iwona, księżniczka Burgundii* (Princess Ivona)—it may be because he lacks the capacity for dramatisation of his own contradictions. He tends instead—as in *Zniewolony umysł,* that fascinating, exasperating, disturbing book—to project onto others the demons he senses in himself. Whence his grim self-satisfaction: he uses self-criticism as a licence to criticise others; he may castigate himself, but he castigates others even more. "Human, all too human" (*CM*), he says as he reviews their compromises and congratulates himself at not having fallen.

E.D. BLODGETT

Miłosz as Witness

Octavio Paz, one of Czesław Miłosz's great predecessors as Charles Eliot Norton Professor at Harvard, concluded his series with the following observation:

> The poetry beginning now, without beginning, is looking for the intersection of times, the point of convergence. It asserts that poetry is the present, between the cluttered past and the uninhabited future. The reproduction is a presentation. Pure time: heartbeat of the presence in the moment of its appearance/disappearance.
>
> (*Children of the Mire*[1])

Miłosz's final word of *The Witness of Poetry* is given to history:

> . . . every day one can see signs indicating that now, at the present moment, something new, and on a scale never witnessed before, is being born: humanity as an elemental force conscious of transcending Nature, for it lives by memory of itself, that is, in History.
>
> (*WP*, 116)

What has happened that in little over a decade two writers such as Paz and Miłosz, sharing the same professorship, should say with unwavering conviction that poetry is known by both its departure from, and re-enty into, history? Has poetry changed or history? And what is there, finally, that poetry possesses that should make its relationship to history so fundamentally imperative? For the imperative is surely the sign beneath which Miłosz's lectures unfold, reminding us unceasingly that poetry is that without which we no longer know who we are or how we should perceive our way through the world's dark wood. Time is not pure for Miłosz, nor is poetry. Thus his lectures are not *explications de texte* nor the history of poetry. They are summoning, as well as a *prise de conscience;* and it requires, as much as a response, a willingness to recognise that poetry may be composed of mere words, but words are the soul's bread.

I confess that I am presenting Miłosz almost as if he were the ghost of another era, as a man whose confidence in poetry is hopelessly out of key with the latter half of the twentieth century. Yet so he signs himself, emphatically framing his lectures with the figure of Poland's Romantic poet, Adam Mickiewicz, of whom he boldly and without apology calls himself a disciple. Nor does it embarrass him at all to define poetry as a "passionate pursuit of the Real" (*WP,* 25). And what is the "Real" if not the recovery, in poetry, of the referential level of discourse, a real that insists upon a "new image of the world, still timidly developing, the one in which the miraculous has a legitimate place." Miłosz's "Real," then is at once a recovery and a response to what may be perceived as the dead end of European poetry of the last 150 years. Not transmuted into transcendent purity, Miłosz's sense of poetry is one that requires a kind of self-recuperation.

Where does the "passionate pursuit of the Real" lead us but into a series of reversals, all of which are calculated to direct our attention towards a re-examination of our past and future? The goal of this re-examination is raised in one essential question: "is noneschatological poetry possible?" (*WP,* 37). If eschatology is not possible, then poetry is not possible. If poetry is not possible, then humanity is not possible. This is the level upon which Miłosz's inquiry rests. To deny its validity leaves poetry where it is for most people (or people who are not poets) and that is on the margin of culture, as if it were a crossword puzzle. If such a poetry were possible, it

> would be a poetry indifferent to the existence of the Past/Future axis and to the "last things"—Salvation and Damnation, Judgement, the King-

> dom of God, the goal of History—in other words, to everything that connects the time assigned to one human life with the time of all humanity.
>
> (*WP*, 37)

At one time it would have been scandalous to raise such a question. To take it seriously again is almost equally scandalous. Why are, we want to ask, poets responsible for God, not to speak of Christian ideology? Nor does Miłosz hesitate to cite Simone Weil who accuses the modernists, and specifically the surrealists, for their "'total absence of value,'" an absence which not only inhibits judgement, but also aligns them against humanity.

What is fundamentally admirable, and somehow persuasive, in what Miłosz is saying is that one has the sense, everywhere in these lectures, that Miłosz has "been there," that he has seen avant gardes come and go, that he has seen through—and lived through—the major political illusions and disillusions of twentieth-century Europe. This does not mean, however, that simply because one is a survivor, as Ortega thought, one has a special knowledge of the significant in literature. Survival requires a kind of "sea-change" and perhaps this is why Ortega's word for survivor—"shipwrecked" (*naufragio*)—is so apt, a word which carries with it a heightened awareness of the fragility of everything one says. Thus Miłosz's lectures are more than a declaration; they are a response, and a response made not so much to the predicament of poetry in the twentieth century and its repeated intimations of apocalypse, as a response to the human predicament to which, as the title of his book eloquently declares, poetry bears witness. Miłosz's point of departure is the sense of utter dead end. We are a wrecked ship, and how are we to find the shore?

In such a context, to speak of the Real, the referential, of values and eschatology seems to appeal to something so enduring in us that perhaps the appeal is not illusory. It is the demonstration of what these terms mean that makes the witness that poetry bears unquestionably convincing. Part of the strength of the demonstration resides in the use of his cousin, Oscar de Milosz, himself a symbolist and therefore, as a poet, part of the dead-centre of the modern, but whose meditations on his contemporaries undermined them as well as himself. For Oscar de Milosz, the poetry of symbolism had lost touch with humanity and, as a result, could not produce a single poet that could witness humanity as Homer, Dante, or Shakespeare. The point of choosing Oscar de Milosz for such a purpose, and as the subject of the second lecture is strategically very clear: Miłosz's own awareness of opposition, contradiction and ambiguity are thus finely displayed, and we know that for him "to be on the side of history" is never a fixed position, for history is never one-sided. Thus poetry is more than a special kind of discourse, it is discourse intimately related to history itself, for, as Oscar de Milosz asserts, "poetry 'appears to us as bound, more rigorously than any other mode of expression, to the spiritual and physical Movement of which it is a generator and a guide'" (*WP*, 25). For Miłosz this means that "the language of every historical period receives its definite shape through poetry" (*WP*, 35). The sign of poetry, then, is Movement, and this would account for Miłosz's antipathy for symbolism whose shadow is everywhere in the modern period, as well as classicism, whose belief in stability and the unchanging it shares.

Part of the point of the overture to Oscar de Milosz is to argue that the flaw in symbolism was evident even to its practioners. Another reason, equally clear, is that Oscar de Milosz serves as a kind of mask for Czesław Miłosz who exposes himself so firmly in the first lecture as a man of divided culture, torn between native origins and Parisian culture. Thus the "self-therapy" that he envisions for twentieth-century poetry acquires a kind of metonymical incarnation in his own work as well as in that of the Polish poetry which is the object of the fifth lecture. So the shape itself of all six lectures from "Starting From My Europe" to "On Hope" provide the scaffold of the argument that runs from self-divisions to closure in hope. The brief anthology of the fifth lecture, combining the themes developed in Oscar de Milosz on poetry and history, serves as an example, and a particularly moving one, of what the new poetry means, and how the act of writing itself depends upon, and is an act of, self-therapy. And this character of the enterprise cannot be overlooked, particularly if we remember that the soul that Miłosz has in mind is not his or that of his fellow-poets, but the soul of Europe emerging from World War Two.

The brilliance of the lecture on Polish poetry resides in the ease with which it overcomes any residual scepticism the reader might feel about the relation of poetry to history, eschatology, referentiality, the Real, the miraculous, and Simone Weil's notion of values. Such poetry is proof, it seems to me at least, that poetry is a witness, particularly in a sense that Miłosz does not explicitly develop. His selection of poems might more properly be called a martyrology, reminding us that the martyr is a witness in a fundamentally eschatological sense, but whose witnessing is, paradox as it may appear, of the human world. For eschatology plays a surprising subtextual role in the transformations of Miłosz's lectures. Where we might think its function is simply Christian in the second lecture, tied as it is to Oscar de Milosz's belief in "the Kingdom of God," by the final lecture its curious secular character begins to take shape. In one stroke Miłosz gathers in modern literature from Shakespeare to "symbolism" as he speaks of a tendency among poets (and not only poets one might add) "to visualize an order located somewhere else, in a different place or time" (*WP*, 107). He then observes: "Such longing, by its nature eschatological, is directed against every 'here and now' and becomes one of the forces contributing to incessant changes" (*WP*, 107). This means the leaning towards final orders is part of the dialectic that not only permits transcendence, but also transforms the world that we do not simply inhabit, but rather continually modify. This returns us to the Real which is the object of our passionate pursuit. The Real is not merely the "here and now." The Real is always mediated. It is what we find in Dostoevsky for whom "reality was multi-layered" (*WP*, 71), and his problem, which re-emerges in Miłosz's notion of the poet, is to discover, in the constantly changing interplay between the eschatological and the "here and now," the Real, if only for a moment. "Otherwise," Miłosz concludes, "as often occurs in contemporary prose-poetry, one finds a 'heap of broken images, where the sun beats,' fragments enjoying perfect equality and hinting at the reluctance of the poet to make a choice" (*WP*, 71). The Real, then requires an order or hierarchy, as Miłosz puts it, as well as the fragments we find lying about us.

The meaning of the Real, however, is not as mystical as it may appear. It is, finally, a poetic event, the event of the poem as witness. For Miłosz this means that all the oppositions with which the lectures begin, the crossroads of Poland that reveal Europe as a division of North and South, East and West, the Past and Future, these oppositions become charged dialectically. Thus the dilemma of the modern poet, inheritor of post-romantic stasis—order without hierarchy—is transmuted. This is the emblematic role that Adam Mickiewicz plays, another figure like Oscar de Milosz through whom oppositions run. Mickiewicz, we find, inherits the Enlightenment, a period of classical order that for Miłosz is analogous to his use of symbolism. Yet in Mickiewicz a crucial event occurs: "the philosophy of *les lumières* is both negated and accepted as a basic optimism toward the future, a millenarian faith in the epoch of the Spirit" (*WP*, 13). This is the exchange that occurs in the dialectic of poetry and history which facilitates the recovery of the relation between poetry and humanity. Without such a recovery, poetry's role as witness is of minimal value.

It is more important to observe, however, that, without saying so explicitly, Miłosz's understanding of Mickiewicz is if not Marxist, at the very least Hegelian. He is more explicit with Oscar de Milosz who not only assisted him in the assimilation of Marxism, but also whose understanding of poetry comes closer to Berthold Brecht than those who write for a more restricted audience. This fact alone, then, should make us sensitive to the eschatological role that Miłosz assigns to poetry. Neither the language of Christianity nor the structures of Marxism stand in opposition to each other for Miłosz: they are rather complementary modes of pursuing the Real, both in touch with the eschatological and both realized in the movement of history. Both, moreover, fail in their charge when history becomes perceived as the past alone. History only has meaning as it bears up on the future, and as it is mediated by the continually transpiring present. Thus for Oscar de Milosz poets such as T.S. Eliot and Ezra Pound, no matter how much we perceive a kind of eschatology in their work, fail to evoke it because of their regressive view of the past. The Real—the eschatological, the referment, the "here and now"—with which poetry is charged, if it is to become witness, is only to be revealed to the degree that poetry participates in history. And in its effort "to make present what is gone by" (*WP*, 114), we are led to the point where history is not realised until it is articulated in verse.

It is clear that Aristotle, who was not a poet, would not have agreed with Miłosz, nor will Miłosz, I fear, find a welcome among those who are of a post-modern persuasion. This is because, I think, he is asking of poetry more than it is normally thought capable of bearing. When poetry becomes a martyrology, we begin to look upon it as a mode of salvation. Or, to put it another way, the renewal that Miłosz requires of poetry is so profoundly implicated with the renewal of the world (in Heidegger's sense) that we must, particularly those of us who are poets, consider very carefully what poetry—and what poets—are for. It is in this sense that Miłosz's book is not merely about poetry. It is a summoning, and it is in response to the book as such that I want to make my concluding remarks.

I want, if only in the most sketchy fashion, to discuss the poetry of Canada and some of the ways in which its contemporary poets have passionately pursued the Real as Miłosz describes. If one were thinking of pure eschatology in an older sense, one might wish to recall the moderns—A.J.M. Smith, Leo Kennedy, A.M. Klein, and, to a certain extent, Jay Macpherson and Margaret Avison. But if I have read Miłosz attentively, my guess is that these are poets, with the possible exception of Klein, who appeal to what Miłosz might call the bohemia of the academy. I hesitate, however, to be definitive, for it is difficult to know how wide the appeal of poetry has ever been in Canada, and whether it is possible to discover a national poet that reaches what Miłosz means by humanity in the way Neruda has, for example, spoken for Chile. In fact, all the poets that I might find grappling with the Real might not even be generally known, and others might know of those who are more appropriate. It is my feeling that the pursuit of the Real is, in any case, rare among our poets for whom either the "here and now" as documentary or the formalism of language is more dominant.

I want to suggest, however, that in English Canada the Real may be found in two or three poets, and in various ways. Of poets of this kind one could not neglect Phyllis Webb whose poetry has been a witness for several decades, and I want to cite one of many poems that possesses the qualities we are seeking called "Treblinka Gas Chamber":

> Klostermayer ordered another count of the children.
> Then their stars were snipped off and thrown into
> the center of the courtyard. It looked like a field
> of buttercups.—Joseph Hyams, *A Field of Buttercups*

fallingstars
'a field of
buttercups'
yellow stars
of David
falling

the prisoners
the children
falling
in heaps
on one another
they go down

Thanatos
showers
his dirty breath
they must breathe
him in

they see stars
behind
their eyes

David's
'a field of
buttercups'
a metaphor
where all that's
left lies down
(*Wilson's Bowl*[2])

It may be, of course, that this is just the kind of poetry that Miłosz argues against, but I do not think that one would accuse it of speaking for a limited audience without concern for human suffering. The Real, however, is not simply suffering, but rather the several ways that the eschatological impinges upon the "here and now." This may be seen in a variety of ways in D.G. Jones whose reach for the Real is mediated by the surprises of Taoism, the particular way in which a certain kind of movement enters his text where

the world keeps
dismantling the syntax,escaping
a final sentence

Penelope weaving
and unweaving,night,day,to
avoid closure
(*Under the Thunder the Flowers Light Up the Earth*[3])

So the future is the present text, continuously open, entering it only to throw it off, such that the Real must be repeatedly pursued and only temporarily caught in poems whose titles are often no more than dates. Finally, I want to cite a poem by Robin Blaser, who must be included in any company of the eschatological, called "A Ceremony":

tenebrae • a true dark of shadows
where we meander among candles
they, one by one, departing from our hearts
unless • we bring them back •

in the cure there are fifteen and then
only one which is hidden in the total dark
of the garden • *strepitus* • the noise
of light • occurs • or wars and turns,
always sudden

(April 1, 1981 (*Syntax*[4]))

How much the date is part of this poem cannot be certain. To fool is not the same as to be ironic, and Blaser's play is almost invariably serious, shuttling us into *tenebrae* and back, always seeking a sign, and always pursuing the syntax of its transmutation.

The poetry of French Canada cannot be thought of without bearing in mind its spiritual bearing. As I have avoided the English Canadian moderns, so I want to avoid their contemporary, Saint-Denys Garneau and direct your attention to Anne Hébert who could almost generally be considered characteristic of the kind of poet we are seeking. This is particularly evident in her *poèmes-en-prose* entitled, *Mystère de la parole.* Most of these are too long to be cited individually, and so I want to restrict myself to the opening stanzas of her marvellous meditation called "Naissance du pain":

> Comment faire parler le pain, ce vieux trésor tout contenu en sa stricte nécessité, pareil à un arbre d'hiver, bien attaché et dessiné, essentiel et nu, contre la transparence du jour?
>
> Si je m'enferme avec ce nom éternel sur mon coeur, dans la chambre noire de mon recueillement, et que je presse l'antique vocable de livrer ses mouvantes images.
>
> J'entends battre contre la porte, lâches et soumises, milles bêtes aigres au pelage terne, aux yeux aveugles; toute une meute servile qui mâchonne des mots comme des herbes depuis les aubes les plus vieilles.
>
> Qu'en ce coeur véhément du poète s'étende donc le claire espace balayé, le long champ de solitude et de dénuement, tandis qu'à l'horizon delivré poindra

parmi les ages décélés, comme de plates pierres bleues
sous la mer, le goût du pain, du sel et de l'eau, à même
la faim millénaire.

(Poèmes[5])

If the symbol of bread were not, of course, transmuted into the Real, Hébert's poem would have foundered in the purely ordinary, but bread that stands as a tree, figured in its essential nudity against the transparence of the day's light permits bread to transcend its almost parochial history to become the bread of anyone. And so bread is not simply discovered in a poem, but, as the title observes, bread is born. This is, perhaps, what we should expect from a poet who observes in the preface to these poems: "je crois à la vertu de la poésie, je crois au salut qui vient de toute parole juste, vécue et exprimée. Je crois à la solitude rompu comme du pain par la poésie." A similar confidence may be seen in the poetry of Hébert's contemporary, Roland Giguère who announces at the beginning of "Continuer à vivre":

S'avancaient sur la nappe mince du présent
un milliers d'images déjà répudiées
et continuaient à nous solliciter ces mirages
d'un monde que nous savions ruiné

et le cancer fleurissait invulnerable

(L'Age de la parole[6])

It is a poem that responds with quick awareness to the problem of twentieth-century despair. But where imagery is ruin and remnant it is possible, as Giguère's poem concludes, for worlds to continue to be invented.

What I am trying to suggest by this choice of poets—and I admit that they may not be enough or even the best choices—is that they each possess in differing ways the special element that Miłosz summons poets to consider. And what strikes one on repeated perusals of these poets is the manner in which they have overcome temptations of self, how the speaker of their poems, individual as it may be, has acquired a voice transcending the isolated ego and, if I may say so, the limited regionality of so many of our poets. The poetry that Miłosz signals as great is great precisely because it has surpassed the small pleasures of yet another psychological insight and speaks to a condition that the world, not the poet, faces. This, it seems to me, is the crux of Miłosz's summoning, the burden that he wants poetry to bear, a burden without which poetry can only become a marginal pastime—a divertimento, in a word.

So the pursuits of poetry continue at several levels of seriousness, but as I write this I am reminded of one of Thomas Merton's remarks. Merton, it can fairly be said, endeavoured with much industry to pursue the Real, and reading Dylan Thomas, he noted once: "Dylan Thomas's integrity as a poet makes me very ashamed of the verses I have been writing." He then went on to remark how depressing it is "that those who serve God and love Him sometimes write so badly, when those who do not believe in Him take pains to write so well" (*The Sign of Jonas*[7]). This, of course, is a just observations, but can one, after all, distinguish writing well from the level of the pursuit? Are there not some pursuits, when pitched at the right level, that begin to design their own curve of excellence? Thus we should, perhaps, modify Merton's comment, for so long as serving God is distinguished from taking pains to write well, there will always be some measure of failure on either side. The burden of Miłosz's enterprise seems to be that the pursuit of the Real which poetry must submit to, and which longs to see "the world which exists objectively—perhaps as it appears in the eyes of God, not as it is perceived by us, desiring and suffering" (*WP*, 115), is an act that emerges on the other side of such qualms as Merton had. The reason is, as Miłosz so decisively argues, that the poem mediates both our world and whatever transcends and thus defines it, and that mediation at a certain point is no longer a problem of writing well, but the manner in which the eschatological chooses to operate. The rest, to modify another phrase, is poetry.

Notes

1. O. Paz, *Children of the Mire: Modern Poetry from Romanticism to the Avant-Garde*, translated by Rachel Phillips (Cambridge, Mass.: Harvard University Press, 1974), p. 164.
2. P. Webb, *Wilson's Bowl* (Toronto: Coach House Press, 1980), p. 43.
3. D.G. Jones, *Under the Thunder the Flowers Light Up the Earth* (Toronto: Coach House Press, 1977), p. 98.
4. R. Blaser, *Syntax* (Vancouver: Talonbooks, 1983), p. 29.

5. A. Hébert, *Poèmes* (Paris: Seuil, 1960), p. 76.
6. R. Giguère, *L'Age de la parole* (Ottawa: Heagone, 1965), p. 105.
7. T. Merton, *The Sign of Jonas* (Garden City, N.J.: Image Books, 1956), p. 66.

EDWARD MOŻEJKO

Miłosz and Post-War Polish Poetry

It is generally believed that the revival of authentic poetic activity in Poland after 1956 was caused by the change of political climate (the so-called "thaw") and the total collapse of the imposed aesthetics of socialist realism which dominated Polish literature between the years 1950–55. While the importance of these factors cannot be denied, it should also be made clear that this evolution constitutes the outer framework only and not the essence of poetic revival itself. In other words, this poetry did not directly reflect political changes themselves[1] (it was not saturated with political messages as it was in other East European countries) but marked primarily a return to the normal life of poetry as art with its vital and principal polemics concerning the task and possible *models* of poetic expression. It should be noted that the beginning of the so-called "thaw" in 1956 coincided with the publication abroad of Czesław Miłosz's *Traktat poetycki* (Poetic Treatise), and inside the country with an increased poetic productivity and critical activity of such poets as Julian Przyboś and Antoni Słonimski. It seems that the younger generation of poets that appeared on the literary scene after 1956, which for convenience is sometimes called the generation of *Współczesność* (Contemporaneity), was more eager to define its position in relation to the tradition of their immediate predecessors than to win the name of political poets. Their poetry was nourished not so much by political events as by poetic programmes and practice which were artificially brought to an end by the imposition of socialist realism in 1949. The range of discussion between 1956 and 1962 included material (both poetic texts and critical essays) that runs from the assessment of the avant-garde of the twenties and the thirties to the revelation of cybernetic poetry of the fifties.[2] Indeed even today, its richness and diversity of artistic standpoints could satisfy the most fastidious lovers of poetry.

By and large, the generation of poets conventionally called "Współczesność" inherited two immediately preceding poetic traditions: that of the Cracow avant-garde, which evolved around the personality of Tadeusz Peiper and was continued after 1945 mainly by Julian Przyboś; and that of the so-called second avant-garde, whose most prominent representative became Czesław Miłosz. Both are distinguishable by some basic characteristics; using semiotic terminology, one can say that the distinctive "sign" of the Cracow avant-garde was its preoccupation with poetic experiment or innovation as beauty an along with it, the cult of technological progress ("miasto, masa, maszyna" ["the city, the masses, the machine"]). In short: the Cracow avant-garde's programme grew out of definite aesthetic premises. The concept of poetry as conceived by Miłosz remains poles apart from what Peiper or Przyboś stood for. It rests on the assumption that the poet is necessarily concerned with man's universal destiny and his culture created throughout centuries of existence. In other words, it places man into relation with his natural existence and at the same time considers him as product of certain cultural, historical traditions. In the final analysis, this duality in Miłosz's is determined by strong *moral* considerations. And it is probably this duality, with its special concern for man's cultural heritage, that has earned him, in the opinion of some critics, the label of being a classicist.[3] Consequently Miłosz's aesthetic proposition combines the two most important spheres of human existence without imposing on them dogmatic limits of interpretation. Hence such a variety of motifs in his poetry exists. They do not contradict each other but are reconciled within a unique poetic ambience. The poetry of Miłosz, more perhaps than the poetry of any other poet of our age, is built on *oppositions*. This dry and somewhat unpoetic term may suggest schematism, but if applied without semiotic rigidity it can be helpful in understanding my point. In the poetry of Miłosz there meets the religious and the human, historical perspective and universal vision, admiration for the age of technology and fear of ecological disaster; there is hope and despair, passion and matter-of-fact reasoning. The philosophical and ethic validity of this poetry was being strengthened as it were, by historical experience. Catastrophism in Miłosz's early poems found its confirmation in the horrors of war. His definite rejection of the "socialist-realist" conception of art further increased his credibility as a writer of dignified status. It also showed that Miłosz did not treat literature as a pastime, but considered poetry to be a vehicle which allowed him to face the most acute issues of modern times.

No wonder that the post-war generation of Polish poets turned their attention towards Miłosz's "Classicism" and found there an almost inexhaustible source of inspiration. The first indication that this poetry would not follow the postulations of the first avant-garde and would turn away from its aestheticism came with the appearance of Różewicz's collection *Niepokój* (Anxiety). However, it will be safe to assume that *Niepokój* originated not so much under the influence of Miłosz as under the pressure of a terrifying reality of the war. But poets who became active after 1956—Z. Herbert, J. Sito, J.M. Rymkiewicz, St. Grochowiak and many others—made no secret as to who their patron was. This phenomenon was promptly noticed by Julian Przyboś, Miłosz's main competitor in the country. He wasted no time in both defending his own understanding of poetry and attacking its adversaries. In a great number of theoretical articles published between the years 1956–1962, Przyboś mostly reaffirmed his old poetic credo, but redistributed the emphasis put on its main components. Now instead of showing his old fascination with technological progress, he stressed the function of poetry as the constant search for beauty, as the ability to "see things anew," in a fresh and unspoiled perception. He called his polemics with the young generation of poets "wojna o piękność"[4] ["a war for beauty"]. Of course, in the given historical situation Przyboś's preoccupation with beauty had a positive aspect too: it could have been interpreted as a sound reaction against the dreadful poetics of socialist realism. However, an attentive reading of these critical articles leaves no doubt whatsoever as to against whom they are directed: we find in them quite a severe attack against the young poets who entered Polish literature in the mid-fifties. These theoretical deliberations were also supported by programmatic statements in poems such as "Oda do turpistów" ("Ode to Turpists"), "Krakowski targ" ("The Cracow's Market"), "Imię czyli odpowiednie rzeczy słowo" ("The Name or the Word Proper of a Thing") and others. But it was not until the beginning of the sixties that Przyboś decided to undertake a direct attack against Miłosz. Obviously, this was due to the growing fascination of young poets with the work of the author of *Traktat poetycki.* In 1960 Jarosław Marek Rymkiewicz published his collection of poetry *Człowiek z głową jastrzębia* (A Man with the Head of a Goshawk) in which such poems as "Do emigranta" ("To an Emigrant"), "Epitafium do mrówki" ("Epitaph to an Ant"), "Ballada" ("Ballad"), "Spinoza był pszczołą" ("Spinoza Was a Bee") were included. They gave a clear indication as to who was gaining the upper hand in the controversy over the essence of modern poetry in Poland. Przyboś responded with a negative review of Rymkiewicz's book. He reproached him for being old-fashioned, artificial, and denounced his device of writing in "stylistic disguise," which meant using old poetic conventions to express modern poetic sensibility. "What is good for the English language in which this tradition is great," wrote Przyboś, "does not mean to be good for Polish."[5] A little bit later in a discussion about literature Przyboś decided to attack the source of Rymkiewicz's inspiration directly and he had the following to say about Miłosz:

> Only one poet, a later emigre, became sincerely preoccupied in his heart and mind with poetry written in English. However, he grazed the avant-garde movement and had the ambition to search for a new style. Miłosz, who translated Eliot's *The Waste Land* and other English and American poets, was so perturbed by Eliot's theory that he advised himself and others to reduce poetic effort to "putting on masks" and use stylization as practiced by Eliot, who reverted to Donne and Vaughan, poets of the seventeenth century. In Miłosz's poetry written abroad, however, one can hardly feel the influence of Eliot's or Auden's poetic language, a language which is almost icy in its precision and play on concepts. Miłosz's style remained as it used to be: stilted declamatory rhetoric. It lacks the play on concepts, what has remained is an old nice-sort-of-chap reasoning. Miłosz tried to imitate not so much the style as the themes raised by Auden and Shapiro. These poets write treaties in verse. Because Shapiro wrote his *Essay on Rime,* Miłosz made his two treaties—one on poetry, the second on morality. It seems to me that they are school-like compositions, a loose discussion about everything and nothing. I do not think that he came even close to his paragon. . . . The monotonous verse

of Miłosz's treaties has no innovative qualities, it sounds pseudoclassical.[6]

However, Przyboś's efforts turned out to be totally futile. Unfortunately, his criticism was not matched by literary practice that would have had any credible appeal for artists, not to say ordinary readers who had always had difficulty appreciating his poetic form and apprehending its message. In the situation where the memories of war were still alive and the country was slowly recovering from the nightmare of Stalinism, Przyboś's call for contemplation of and search for beauty sounded like the confessions of a naive man who did not comprehend what had happened. Such confessions remained in ironic discordance with the realities of life. Even less convincing were his projections about the art of the future. In the article "Jaka będzie sztuka przyszłości" ("What Will Be the Art of the Future") Przyboś predicted a constant "modernization" or "renovation" of poetry which would reflect the evergrowing spiritual self-improvement of man. Future poetry would not extol what already exists but it will sing dithyrambs to honour the future. Modern poetry will constantly revolutionize the human imagination and substitute for existing beauty or the beauty to come. This programme never implied any questioning of reality as a tragic phenomenon filled with unhappiness and moral conflicts. In the context of these programmatic deliberations, "Oda do turpistów" becomes more understandable. It was an artistic endorsement of theoretical claims. In it Przyboś condemned the existing cult of ugliness (Latin "turpis," "turpe") that was spreading through many poems (especially those of St. Grochowiak) written by younger poets—a trend exactly opposite to what he advocated.

Przyboś's theoretical statements and poems sparked an avalanche of responses in the form of both poetic texts and critical articles. The common denominator in all these pronouncements was a call for expressing meaning in poetry instead of immersing in intricate speculations about a notion as abstract as beauty. It is interesting to note statements made by established poets such as A. Słonimski and T. Różewicz. In his "List otwarty" ("Open Letter"),[8] the former member of the *Skamander* group complained that under the sign-board of modernity we often encounter an incredible indigence of thought, and that the complicated poetic language of many modernists reflects nothing but lack of talent.

As an antidote to this illness in literature, Słonimski recommended to

Polish poets that they avail themselves of the experience of their Anglo-American colleagues such as C. Sandburg, T.S. Eliot. W.H. Auden, S. Spender and others. In his demand for clarity and meaning in poetry, he came close to defending the position of Miłosz.

T. Różewicz's most important contribution to the polemics with Przyboś was a short poem entitled "Uzasadnienie" ("Justification").[9] It is a short philosophical "treatise" about the essence of poetic expression. He rejects Przyboś's idea of "wholeness" which would give a well-calculated and "neat" presentation of the world. Instead, he defends concreteness in poetry and fragmentation or atomization of expression.

Rzecz obraz
zdarzenie
dopiero izolowane
odcięte zamknięte
stają się jasne
ostre wyraźne
i zbliżone
nie "do prawdy"
lecz do siebie

("Uzasadnienie")

A thing image
event
when isolated
cut off and closed
becomes clear
sharp distinct
and close
not to "truth"
but to itself

("Justification," tr. E.M.)

wrote Różewicz in the opening lines of his poem.

The most uncompromising rejection of Przyboś's model of poetry came from young poets. They also made perfectly clear whom they considered to be their aesthetic patron. The most forceful criticism of Przyboś was formulated by Ireneusz Iredyński in his poem "Traktat o kazaniu"[10] ("A

Treatise on Sermon"), the title of which bore a clear affinity with Miłosz's *Traktat poetycki.* The following quotations from Irdyński's poem speak for themselves and actually do not require any comments:

Czas awangardę ze Skamander pogodził
Skamander był ptakiem co śpiewał przed nożem
Awangarda szybka w chacie pobielonej
w której odbijały chmury jak konstrukcje
Kamień strzaskał szybkę
Świadomych było tylko paru z Wilna
mieli czas pomyśleć iż człowiek jest z mięsa
tylko ich wiersze bite czcionką z ognia
i tylko oni nie są zakłamani

Więc awangardzista dzisiaj znów gromi
chłopców co mieli poprzedników w Wilnie
którzy wiedzą iż wojna krematoria bomby
są poza Estetyką I w czasie pokoju
chwalą brzydotę nie Konwencję Piękna
To jest ich obrona ta brzydota zwykła
która jest teraz—tak! pięknem jedynym
i to jest ta jedna drobina godności

("Traktat o kazaniu")

The time has reconciled Skamander to Avant-Garde
Skamander was a bird which sang under the knife
The Avant-Garde passed quickly among white-painted huts
on which the clouds, like constructions, were reflected
The stone shattered the window-pane
Only a few in Vilno were aware
and had time to think that man is made of flesh
only their poems were printed in type made of fire
and only they are not mendacious.

So today the avant-gardist reproves again
the boys who have their predecessors in Vilno
who know that war crematories bombs
are beyond Aesthetics; And in time of peace
they praise not the Convention of Beauty but ugliness

That ordinary ugliness is their defence
which exists now—yes! the only beauty
their only particle of pride
("A Treatise on Sermon," tr. E.M.)

Iredyński concluded his poem with a bitter malicious statement that Przyboś has no followers:

Mój zacny proboszczu aby kogoś gromić trzeba mieć parafię
("Traktat o kazaniu")

My respectable rector in order to reprove someone you ought to have
a parish
("A Treatise on Sermon," tr. E.M.)

The greatest impact exercised by Miłosz on Polish post-war poetry was on the so-called "classicists": Z. Herbert, J. Sito, J.M. Rymkiewicz, A. Międzyrzecki and others. In his book on Classicism, R. Przybylski, speaking of J. Sito, remarked that this poetry *as that of any* poet in the classicist stream "went through the school of Czesław Miłosz."[11]

Virtually any poet of the post-1956 generations can claim an affinity with Miłosz, whether representing turpism, Classicism or the catholicism of the *Tygodnik Powszechny* group. Those who desired to "speak straightforwardly" could refer to Miłosz's courage to bring up the controversial and tragic questions of our time; and those who were inclined to "speak in disguise" by using stylistic imitation might point to Miłosz's respect and admiration for the Judeo-Christian cultural, religious and literary tradition.

Finally, I should mention the most recent manifestation of Miłosz's influence on Polish poets. I have in mind the poem "Drzewo" ("The Tree") by Marek Skwarnicki,[12] a poet closely associated with the catholic group of *Tygodnik Powszechny* in Cracow. The poem can be interpreted as a philosophical treatise on Poland's historical and cultural destiny, about a country that is tragically caught in between its geographic location as an East European country and its tradition that ties it closely to the West. Here is the opening sestina of the poem:

W mojej ojczyźnie, we wschodniej Europie
pomiędzy stepem i ruiną Rzymu,

na szczycie wzgórza drzewo stoi złote,
dołem, po rżysku pełznie smuga dymu
i wiatr odpina liście z dekoracji,
Którą tak lubią w poezji Polacy.

("Drzewo")

In my fatherland, in Eastern Europe
between the steppes and the ruins of Rome,
on the top of a hill stands a golden tree,
in the valley on the rye stubble smoke drifts
and the wind undoes the leaves of decoration,
Which is so beloved by the Poles.

("The Tree," tr. E.M.)

Skwarnicki's poem brings up the question of national or even personal identity and the choices that such identity may force individuals to make. It is a theme constantly present in the whole of Miłosz's literary work. It does not take an ear for music to recognize that Skwarnicki's poem recalls the intonation of Miłosz's "W mojej ojczyźnie" and in fact it constitutes its poetic paraphrase (compare with p. 6 of this book) which unfolds a sequence of images referring to Polish history, literature and contains direct mention of Miłosz. Its pensive tone reflects apprehension as to the future of Poland.

In this paper I have only touched upon the proverbial "tip of the iceberg." I hope my discussion sparks a more detailed investigation of this important topic. K. Wyka called J. Tuwim "drzewo poezji polskiej" ["the tree of Polish poetry"]. The history of Polish poetry in the past forty years seems to suggest that it would be much more appropriate to apply this qualification to Miłosz.

Notes

1. This does not mean that political poetry did not exist. It is sufficient to mention A. Ważyk's poem "Poemat dla dorosłych."
2. M. Mazur, "Cybernetyka a sztuka," *Nowa kultura,* nr. 27 (1962).

3. M. Janion, "To jest klasycyzm tragiczny," introduction to R. Przybylski's book *To jest klasycyzm* (Warsaw: Czytelnik, 1978), p. 10.
4. J. Przyboś, "Do Młodych," *Przegląd kulturalny*, nr. 41 (1960).
5. For the original see J. Przyboś, "List do młodego poety," *Przegląd kulturalny*, nr. 51 (1960). [Translation by E. Możejko.]
6. For the original see J. Przyboś in "Dyskusja o literaturze," *Przegląd kulturalny*, nr. 33 (1960). [Translation by E. Możejko.]
7. J. Przyboś, "Jaka będzie sztuka przyszłości" *Nowa kultura*, nr. 45 (1961).
8. A. Słonimski, "List otwarty," *Nowa kultura*, nr. 14 (1961). See also his poem "W obronie wiersza," *Nowa kultura*, nr. 2 (1961).
9. T. Różewicz, "Uzasadnienie," *Przegląd kulturalny*, nr. 51–52 (1958).
10. In R. Przybylski, *To jest klasycyzm* (Warsaw: Czytelnik, 1978), p. 241.
11. For the original see ibid., p. 97. Author's emphasis added.
12. M. Skwarnicki, "Drzewo" in the collection *Zmierzch* (Cracow: Wydawnictwo Literackie, 1979), pp. 47–56. The poem was published in the winter of 1971–72 in *Tygodnik Powszechny*.

APPENDIX: CZESŁAW MIŁOSZ'S APPEARANCES IN CANADA

ANNA BIOLIK

Miłosz in Ottawa

February 13, 1984

An open mind, appreciation of poetry and a ticket were all that one needed to participate in an interesting, entertaining and elegant evening listening to Nobel Laureate Czesław Miłosz. The event took place on February 13, 1984 and was sponsored by the Department of Modern Languages and Literatures at the University of Ottawa, with the cooperation of the Canadian-Polish Congress. It was organized by Professor Anna Biolik who was in charge of the Polish Programme in the Slavic Section at the time of the poet's visit to Ottawa.

Due to local publicity, including articles in the *Ottawa Citizen* and the two university publications, *The Fulcrum* and *Gazette*,[1] a large number of invitations being sent and word of mouth, the evening was very well attended. The audience consisted of professors from a wide variety of disciplines, distinguished members of the community, students, as well as a myriad of other poetry-enthusiasts.

The audience also reflected the multi-lingual aspect of Miłosz's poetry. He composes his material primarily in Polish, although his works are usually translated into English and French. Originally, Miłosz was considered to be "untranslatable." "The poetry was known to be 'the main thing,' but seemed to be completely language-bound," stated John Carpenter in his article in "Books from Borders."[2] Nonetheless a co-operative effort of several people including poets and translators has made it possible to find Miłosz's poetry published in English and French. Miłosz also proved himself to be fluent in both of these languages and alternated between the three throughout the evening.

Miłosz was known as one of the "catastrophists," a name tagged onto a kind of poet who, largely due to the pervading atmosphere of imminent disaster in the late 1930s were profoundly affected by the constant threat of war and whose poetry greatly reflected this state of mind. One of the poems Miłosz included in his repertoire was "Piosenka o końcu świata" ("A Song on the End of the World"):

> A którzy czekali błyskawic i gromów,
> Są zawiedzeni.
> . . . .
> Dopóki trzmiel nawiedza różę,
> Dopóki dzieci różowe się rodzą,
> Nikt nie wierzy, że staje się już.
> ("Piosenka o końcu świata," *UP,* 95)

> And those who expected lightning and thunder
> Are disappointed.
> . . . .
> As long as the bumblebee visits a rose,
> As long as rosy infants are born
> No one believes it is happening now.
> ("A Song on the End of the World," *SP,* 57)

However Miłosz is also a poet who is interested in a diverse array of subjects. In his *Nobel Lecture,* Miłosz tried to answer a question which is constantly on his mind:

> What is this enigmatic impulse that does not allow one to settle down in the achieved, the finished? I think it is a quest for reality.

It is through his search for reality, or rather his constant dialogue with reality, that Miłosz's poetry gains its particular significance. In his poetry we are looking not only for a kind of "lyrical" emotion or feeling, but for a truth which, with the accuracy of its prophetic power, lets us discover the uniqueness of Miłosz's verse and its specificity which stems from a particular dialectical tension between imagination and reality, past and present, poetical form and its diction. In one of his poems, "Ars poetica?", he states:

> Ten pożytek z poezji, że nam przypomina
> jak trudno jest pozostać tą samą osobą,
> bo dom nasz jest otwarty, na drzwiach nie ma klucza
> a niewidzialni goście wchodzą i wychodzą.
>
> ("Ars poetica?" *UP*, 316)

> The purpose of poetry is to remind us
> how difficult it is to remain just one person,
> for our house is open, there are no keys in the doors,
> and invisible guests come in and out at will.
>
> ("Ars poetica?" *BW*, 31)

Another theme of his poetry primarily reflects his own situation, that of a "poet in exile," a point I emphasized in my introduction to the audience. Miłosz is one of those rare poets who not only belongs to the category of poets in exile trying to pinpoint what his position of being a foreigner means, a position which turns out to be one of the principal characteristics of man's situation today, but also he is one who continues to create while exiled. And what is even more exceptional, to create in his native tongue.[3]

Notes

1. See *The Ottawa Citizen,* February 16, 1984; *The Fulcrum* 21 (1984); and *Gazette* 19, no. 1 (February 1, 1984).
2. "Books from borders," *A Book Review* IV, no. IV (April–May), pp. 1–2.
3. It should be noted that Dr. A. Biolik kindly provided the information about Miłosz's visit to Montreal. The author of *Zniewolony umysł (The Captive Mind)* was invited by the Polish Institute of Arts and Sciences in Canada on the occasion of the fortieth anniversary of its foundation in Montreal on May 3, 1983. On May 4th he was interviewed by Radio Canada. All the material about Miłosz's sojourn in Montreal is available in a special brochure, published by the Institute under the title *Czesław Miłosz* (1983). It contains a presentation of Miłosz by Professor Wladimir Krysiński, reprinted articles from the Montreal *Gazette, Le Devoir* and the above-mentioned interview.

MARK KLUS

Czesław Miłosz in Toronto

March 24–25, 1977

Czesław Miłosz came to Toronto towards the end of March 1977. At that time we knew him mainly as the author of *The History of Polish Literature.* When I asked Professor Louis Iribarne of the University of Toronto in his course on Polish culture and civilization shortly before the visit how he rated Miłosz among the contemporary Polish writers, he placed him at the top. I then asked, "Of those living outside Poland?" He replied, "No, of those outside *and* inside." A few eyebrows were raised on hearing this.

The first item on Miłosz's three-day agenda was an evening lecture in Polish with the English title "Poet Between East and West." It was given in a lecture hall filled with eager listeners. At the time I understood little Polish, probably most of those who did had a hard enough time understanding him as it was because of the concentrated train of complex thoughts expressed in a seemingly simple language. Miłosz impressed me right off as being a rather spry sixty-five years of age, his hair being a mixture of brown and iron-gray with a cowlick. Only his crease-lined face gave his age away, and those now famous owlish eyebrows. A certain boyish quality showed itself when he would stop his reading for a moment, remove his large, plastic, square-rimmed glasses and expand on a point. At the beginning, after an introduction in Polish by Iribarne, he promised to read and not improvise but as the reading progressed a certain impassioned zeal made itself felt in frequent minor digressions in which he tried to make his main point clear; reality in the shape of a faceless, indifferent totalitarianism facing man in the twentieth century is becoming more and more threatening and at the same time more and more difficult to name. The burden on the poet is to somehow express this reality, yet he is also morally compromised because of an inhumane, cruel distance that a true artist must maintain towards himself and others. This lecture appeared in Polish with the title of "Niemoralność sztuki" ("Immorality of Art"). Miłosz may have appeared here as a late descendant of Thomas Mann's Tonio Kröger (from whom he took his cue), but he was a Tonio Kröger of enormous energy.

The next day Iribarne had Miłosz over to the Slavic Department for a noon-hour discussion over tea and cookies (which Miłosz devoured with gusto) with a few members of the staff and some dozen students. Topics from the wide-ranging talk that stood out were Miłosz's explanation (at Iribarne's behest) of his view of *Pan Tadeusz* as a metaphysical poem written as a compensation, as it were, for Conrad's Promethean rebellion (similar to Ivan Karamazov's) against God; the difficulty of Gombrowicz's "Ślub" ("Marriage") which a student wanted to stage was remarked upon; the Polish-Western social and political situation was discussed as well with Miłosz maintaining that a *Zniewolony umysł (The Captive Mind)* vis-a-vis the West needed to be written and, more interestingly, that were the Iron Curtain to fall Poland would become a Westernized country in a day, a proposition he did not relish: "We must find a third way."

For me the real Miłosz, a rather more than lyrical and spellbinding one, appeared late that afternoon to give a bilingual reading of his poetry with Iribarne as co-reader and introducer at the hallowed halls of Hart House. Unfortunately, fifty people at most were in attendance, a pitiful number the time of day notwithstanding. Iribarne spoke of Miłosz as going through "a kind of second debut" for North American audiences and read the poems in English, while Miłosz read them in the original Polish with a short commentary in English preceding a new poem. He began with "Greek Portrait" in English and then in Polish "Portret grecki." It did not take long for a kind of magical aura to settle over the gathering. Lines speaking of the "human heart holding more than speech does" betraying a certain keen yet humble awareness of reality caught my attention at once. When Miłosz switched to Polish an urgency and rhythmic power suddenly became more palpable: "Brodę mam gęstą, oczy przesłonięte / Powieką." Poetry is meant to be spoken aloud and here was living proof since, for this listener at least, poetry, art itself came to life as it were. Miłosz literally sang through "Piosenka o końcu świata" ("A Song on the End of the World") and made it into an incantation. Here was a real poet who spoke with authority. Out of the twenty poems presented, the most popular in terms of applause were in English: "Greek Portrait," "To Raja Rao" (the only original English poem of Miłosz's), "A Song on the End of the World," "Ars Poetica?" and "Wieść" ("Tidings"). At the same time a vein of humour ran throughout the reading that was in turn reflective, tragic pathetic, thus giving Miłosz and his poetry a balanced and closer-to-life quality. This persisted to the end when Miłosz was asked his view of existence and essence: "I don't know what it [existentialism] is." A moment of wheezy laughter was followed by a more serious answer: "Let us say that in the twentieth century we have a great longing for essence. Not always it is possible, but I have a great propensity in this direction. I do not deny it." After this overall revelation Iribarne's high opinion of Miłosz no longer seemed so exaggerated.

October 24–26, 1980

Miłosz's next visit to Toronto, just after he received the Nobel Prize, was an altogether different affair, not so much for the Polish-speaking community who knew who they had, but for the larger public. First, though, Miłosz (after a standing ovation accorded him on his arrival) took part on Friday evening in a panel discussion that opened a conference on Poles in North America. The panel, composed of writers and academics, gave their views on various aspects on the (non-)integration of Poles into North America society. Miłosz, who had no text, spoke briefly but movingly with a look of pained intensity (lowered, furrowed brows, face flushed with emotion) on the "enormous zones of silence" covering the fates of thousands of Polish immigrants who sacrificed their lives for their children in uncertainty, poverty and anonymity. Their history needed to be written, he felt, not only from the side of high-brow literature which he had partially accomplished in his *History of Polish Literature*, but from a more immediate point of contact with these people as shown by the example of Louis Adamic. (Miłosz's poem "Pamięci Teresy Żarnower" ("In Memory of Teresa Żarnower") written in 1949 may be recalled in connection with these problems.) The entire proceedings of this round table were published in 1983 by the Canadian Polish Research Institute (CPRI) in Toronto under the title of *Polishness*.

On Saturday evening Miłosz appeared at the International Authors' Festival organized by Greg Gatenby at Toronto's Harbourfront. This time the attendance was closer to five hundred. However, since Miłosz shared the podium with three other authors, his programme was a short one. Even so it possessed a different character than usual since he and Iribarne read sections in Polish and English from *Dolina Issy (The Issa Valley)* ("a rather roguish novel") (chapters 1—landscape and setting, 2—introduction of devils, 40—the hunt) which for some seemed a little overloaded with imagery and description for a reading of this sort. When Miłosz returned to his poetry, the usual staple of war poems was included due to audience demand—"Przedmowa" ("Dedication"), "A Song on the End of the World," "Biedny chrześcijanin . . ." ("A Poor Christian . . .") along with "To Raja Rao" tacked on as an afterthought. Overall, Miłosz seemed a little nervous at this reading. Small wonder, for how was one to cope with all this sudden, well-meant but misdirected adulation.

Next afternoon, a Sunday, however, he was in top form and at home in his native Polish at the Trinity College chapel at the University of Toronto. On the new agenda this time were not his poems but his translations from Greek and Hebrew of parts of the Old Testament which he had been working on for several years. Miłosz dedicated the reading to his recently deceased close friend and collaborator on these translations, Father Józef Sadzik, and this lent a melancholy flavour to an already intense atmosphere. In the introduction he also listed his reasons for undertaking such a task: return to the sources of his poetry, return to the roots of the Polish language, reaction to the unsatisfactory contemporary translations, search for a new kind of hieratic but unarchaic Polish. A foundation was built as it were with a selection of over a dozen Psalms into which fragments from the *Song of Songs*, the *Book of Job*, the *Lamentations of Jeremiah* and *Ecclesiastes* were inserted at various intervals. The reading lasted a little over an hour but in terms of quality I had never heard contemporary language employed on such a sublime, clear, dignified and at times severe level as here. Often Miłosz would point to numerous points in common between the history of Israel in Biblical times and history of modern Poland. In some ways this reading superseded that of 1977 because the Biblical passages chosen had an archetypal significance that for once shone through in translation whether they were hymns of praise, laments, complaints, bitter reflections or songs of love. It was an unforgettable experience. In an interview given by Miłosz for CBC radio, the main topics of discussion were contemporary Polish poetry and Miłosz's part in it as author and translator. Also mentioned was yet another reason for his Biblical translations: the need for a purification on the part of Poles from the genocidal crimes which have sullied their land. In addition a shorter talk with Sam Solecki was broadcast which, however, I was not able to hear.

September 10–11, 1982

In 1982 the annual Toronto International Film Festival showed Tadeusz Konwicki's film version of *The Issa Valley*. Miłosz was scheduled to see it at a private viewing on Friday and participate Saturday afternoon in a panel discussion of writers whose work was represented at the Festival. His reaction to the film was understandably negative since it had more to do with Konwicki's perception of reality than with Miłosz. Much of the film was too dreamlike as opposed to the rock-hard concrete details in which Miłosz revelled. He objected most of all to the cursory treatment of Thomas, the misunderstanding of Balthazar's character ("He is a philosopher, not a madman") and to the interjection of scenes extraneous to the novel. Yet despite all this and more he did sympathize with his fellow countryman Konwicki in regarding the film as a "cri de coeur" for their lost Lithuanian-Polish homeland.

The panel discussion at the Harbourfront that included contributions by Margaret Atwood, Timothy Findley and Roger Lemelin, was divided into two parts, the first dealing with panel's reflections on the two media of literature and film. Miłosz compared the two in terms of capturing doses of reality in varying degrees, and also spoke of the general failure of films to capture the spirit of the literary works on which they were based. The second, more interesting part consisted of the panel reading selections from their own works. It was not surprising that Miłosz chose to read (with Iribarne) selections from *The Issa Valley*. This time, though, they found a better solution in taking only a paragraph or two from various chapters, thus rendering them easier for the audience of 150 people to absorb. There was humour in abundance: early on Iribarne was reading a passage that mentioned thunder when at once some strange, banging sounds were heard in the rafters to which Miłosz automatically pointed with a big grin. He spoke of the novel as being "extremely erotic" and proceeded to read of Thomas's moment of ecstatic revelation with the ermine at the end of chapter six, and of using animals to describe human characteristics, namely his own. He illustrated this point with the short passage from the final chapter comparing the two horses, hard-working Smilga and lazy, impatient Birnik. Presented in this fashion the short fragments were almost miniature poems. This concluded Miłosz's public appearance in Toronto.

EDWARD MOŻEJKO

Miłosz in Edmonton

February 23–25, 1972

Czesław Miłosz visited Edmonton twice. In 1972 (February 23–25) his visit was sponsored by the Committee on Soviet and East European Studies, the Department of Comparative Literature at the University of Alberta and the Polish Cultural Society in Edmonton. He delivered two lectures: "Literature in a post-Marxist situation" and "Man against form." In his third public appearance at the University of Alberta, he read his poetry.

September 14–15, 1981

Miłosz's second visit to Edmonton was different in scope. He arrived as a celebrity, i.e., as a Nobel Prize Winner for literature, on September 14–15, 1981. This visit was officially proclaimed by its organizers, the Polish Cultural Society in Edmonton, with the cooperation of the University of Alberta, as "Miłosz Days in Edmonton."

The Polish community and the University milieu in Edmonton reacted very enthusiastically to Miłosz's distinction by the Swedish Academy. Shortly after the media announced the news, the *Edmonton Journal* on October 18, 1980 published an article by E. Możejko, "Nobel prize no surprise to his fans." Readings of Miłosz's poetry were organized on the campus and lectures about his poetry were addressed to some local Polish organizations. This series of events culminated in the September, 1981 "Miłosz

Days in Edmonton," probably a unique event on the North American Continent.

The programme of "Miłosz Days in Edmonton" was rich in content: it included an exhibition of Miłosz's books in the University library, publication of a poster commemorating "Miłosz Days in Edmonton" (projected and artistically implemented by Mr. Jan Tereszczenko), sale of Miłosz's collected works published by *Kultura* in Paris and other books (mainly translations), an evening with the Polish community (at the Polish Hall), a lunch with local Canadian writers, interviews with Polish television ("Polonica"), Canadian TV (French Program) and the *Edmonton Journal* (James Adams).

A special symposium devoted to Miłosz writings was organized and scholars from other universities were invited to participate.[1] The most impressive event of these celebrations took place on the evening of September 15th when Miłosz read his poetry in the Convocation Hall of the Old Arts Building. Gathered together were over three hundred listeners: professors, students, Poles living in Edmonton and the public at large. The encounter with Miłosz's poetry was best characterized by a student of comparative literature, who said that he was "shaken by this unforgettable experience."

Notes

1. See a detailed discussion of "Miłosz Days" in E. Możejko's article "'Dni Miłosza' w Edmonton," *Dialogi—Dialogues* I, no. 1 (1984): 22–23.

Czesław Miłosz signing autographs at the Polish Hall, Edmonton, Alberta, September 14, 1981. In the background are Prof. Madeline Levine, Prof. Edward Możejko and Dr. Henryk Wójcicki, President of the Polish Canadian Congress, Alberta Branch at the time of the event.

Czesław Miłosz (left) in conversation with Prince Piotr Czartoryski (centre) and retired University of Alberta librarian Adam Kantautas (right), September 15, 1981.

Czesław Miłosz (centre) visiting the exhibition devoted to his writing at Rutherford Library South, University of Alberta, September 15, 1981. Surrounding Prof. Miłosz (from left to right) are Mrs. Ewa Jakobs, Prof. Bogdan Czaykowski, Prof. Edward Możejko, Ms. Ewa Wadolna and Ms. Teresa Ignasiak.

Czesław Miłosz at the exhibition of his writings, organized by the University Library, University of Alberta, September 15, 1981.

A LIST OF CZESŁAW MIŁOSZ'S BOOKS

Books in Polish

Człowiek wśród skorpionów: studium o Stanisławie Brzozowskim. Paris: Instytut Literacki, 1962.

Dolina Issy. Paris: Instytut Literacki, 1955. [*The Issa Valley*. Translated by Louis Iribarne. New York: Farrar Straus Giroux, 1981.]

Gdzie wschodzi słońce i kędy zapada. Paris: Instytut Literacki, 1974.

Gucio zaczarowany. Paris: Instytut Literacki, 1965.

Hymn o perle. Ann Arbor: Michigan Slavic Publications, 1980.

Kontynenty. Paris: Instytut Literacki, 1958.

Król Popiel i inne wiersze. Paris: Instytut Literacki, 1962.

Kroniki: Nowy tom poezji. Paris: Instytut Literacki, 1987.

Księga Hioba. Paris: Editions du dialogue, 1981.

Księga psalmów. Paris: Editions du dialogue, 1979.

Księgi pięciu megilot. Paris: Editions du dialogue, 1982.

Miasto bez imienia. Paris: Instytut Literacki, 1969.

Nieobjęta ziemia. Paris: Instytut Literacki, 1984.

Ocalenie. Warsaw: Czytelnik, 1945.

Odczyt w Akademii Szwedzkiej. [Nobel Lecture.] New York: Farrar Straus Giroux, 1981.

Ogród nauk. Paris: Instytut Literacki, 1979.

Poemat o czasie zastygłym. Wilno: Koło Polonistów Słuchaczy Uniwersytetu Stefana Batorego, 1933.

Poezje, Vol. I–III. Paris: Instytut Literacki, 1981–82.

Po stronie dialogu. Warsaw: PIW, 1983.

Prywatne obowiązki. Paris: Instytut Literacki, 1972.

Rodzinna Europa. Paris: Instytut Literacki, 1959. [*Native Realm: A Search for Self-Definition.* New York: Doubleday, 1968.]

Świadectwo poezji: sześć wykładów o dotkliwości naszego wieku. Paris: Instytut Literacki, 1983. [*The Witness of Poetry.* Cambridge, Mass.: Harvard University Press, 1983.]

Światło dzienne. Paris: Instytut Literacki, 1953.

Traktat poetycki. Paris: Instytut Literacki, 1957.

Trzy zimy & Głosy o wierszach—eseje. Edited by Renata Gorczyńska and Piotr Kłoczowski. London: Aneks Publishers, 1987.

Trzy zimy. Poezje. Warsaw-Wilno: Związek Zawądowy Literatów Polskich, 1936.

Utwory poetyckie. Poems. Ann Arbor: Michigan Slavic Publications, 1976.

Widzenia nad zatoką San Francisco. Paris: Instytut Literacki, 1969. [*Visions from San Francisco Bay.* New York: Farrar Straus Giroux, 1982.]

Wiersze. Cracow: Wydawnictwo Literackie, 1985.

Wiersze. London: Oficyna Poetów i Malarzy, 1967.

Wiersze wybrane. Warsaw: PIW, 1980.

Zaczynając od moich ulic. Paris: Instytut Literacki, 1985.

Zdobycie władzy. Paris: Instytut Literacki, 1953. [*The Seizure of Power.* Translated by Celina Wieniawska. New York: Criterion Books, 1955.]

Ziemia Ulro. Paris: Instytut Literacki, 1977. [*The Land of Ulro.* New York: Farrar Straus Giroux, 1984.]

Zniewolony umysł. Paris: Instytut Literacki, 1953. [*The Captive Mind.* Translated by Jane Zielonko. New York: Knopf, 1953.]

Books in English

Bells in Winter. Translated by the author and Lillian Valee. New York: The Ecco Press, 1978.

The Captive Mind. Translated by Jane Zielonko. New York: Knopf, 1953. [*Zniewolony umysł.* Paris: Instytut Literacki, 1953.]

The Collected Poems, 1931–1987. New York: The Ecco Press, 1988.

Emperor of the Earth: Modes of Eccentric Vision. Berkeley: University of California Press, 1977.

The History of Polish Literature. New York: Macmillan, 1969.

The Invincible Song: A Clandestine Anthology. Ann Arbor: University of Michigan Press, 1981.

The Issa Valley. Translated by Louis Iribarne. New York: Farrar Straus Giroux, 1981. [*Dolina Issy.* Paris: Instytut Literacki, 1955.]

The Land of Ulro. New York: Farrar Straus Giroux, 1984. [*Ziemia Ulro.* Paris: Instytut Literacki, 1977.]

Native Realm: A Search for Self-Definition. New York: Doubleday, 1968. [*Rodzinna Europa.* Paris: Instytut Literacki, 1959.]

Postwar Polish Poetry: An Anthology. Garden City, N.J.: Doubleday, 1968.

The Seizure of Power. Translated by Celina Wieniawska. New York: Criterion Books, 1955. [*Zdobycie władzy.* Paris: Instytut Literacki, 1953.]

Selected Poems. Translated by Kenneth Rexroth. New York: The Seabury Press, 1973. [Rev. ed. New York: The Ecco Press, 1981.]

The Separate Notebooks. Translated by Robert Hass and Robert Pinsky with the author and Renata Gorczyński. New York: The Ecco Press, 1984.

Unattainable Earth. Translated by the author and Robert Hass. New York: The Ecco Press, 1986.

Visions from San Francisco Bay. New York: Farrar Straus Giroux, 1982. [*Widzenia nad zatoką San Francisco.* Paris: Instytut Literacki, 1969.]

The Witness of Poetry. Cambridge, Mass.: Harvard University Press, 1983.

SELECTED BIBLIOGRAPHY OF LITERARY CRITICISM ON CZESŁAW MIŁOSZ

Adams, James. "Continuing the long, strange journey. (Nobel Prize winner visits Edmonton)." *Edmonton Journal*, September 16, 1981, section H, p. 2.

Barańczak, Stanisław. "A Black Mirror at the End of A Tunnel: An Interpretation of Czesław Miłosz's 'Świty'." *The Polish Review* XXXI, no. 4 (1986), pp. 276–84.

Bereś, Stanisław. "Rozważania nad programem Żagarów." *Pamiętnik literacki* LXXV, no. 2(1984), pp. 93–133.

Błoński, Jan. "Muzyka późnych lat albo o formie moralnej." *Tygodnik powszechny* 27(1986), p. 3.

Bolecki, Włodzimierz. "Proza Miłosza." *Pamiętnik literacki* LXXV, no. 2(1984), pp. 133–66.

Chrząstkowska, Bożena. *Poezje Czesława Miłosza.* Warsaw: Wydawnictwa Szkolne i Pedagogiczne, 1982.

Czarnecka, Ewa. *Podróżny świata.* New York: Bicentennial Publishing Company, 1983.

———, and Aleksander Fiut. *Conversations with Czesław Miłosz*, translated by Richard Lourie. San Diego: Harcourt Brace Jovanovich, 1987.

Davie, Donald. *Czesław Miłosz and the Insufficiency of Lyric.* Knoxville: University of Tennessee Press, 1986.

Dompkowski, Judith Ann. "Down a Spiral Staircase, Never-Ending: Motion as Introduction to Czesław Miłosz." Ph.D. dissertation, State University of New York at Buffalo, 1983.

Dybciak, Krzysztof. "Tak czytano Miłosza." *Przegląd powszechny* IV (1986), pp. 63–73.

Fiut, Aleksander. "Reading Miłosz." *The Polish Review* XXXI, no. 4(1986), pp. 257–64.

———. *Rozmowy z Czesławem Miłoszem.* Cracow: Wydawnictwo Literackie, 1981.

Kijowski, Andrzej. "Tematy Miłosza." *Twórczość* XXXVII, no. VI (1981), pp. 33–44.

Kwiatkowski, Jerzy, ed. *Poznawanie Miłosza: studia i szkice o twórczości poety.* Cracow: Wydawnictwo Literackie, 1985.

Łapiński, Zdzisław. *Między polityką a metafizyką: o poezji Czesława Miłosza.* London: Odnowa, 1981.

Mazur, Marian. "Cybernetyka a sztuka." *Nowa kultura* 27(1962) 10–11.

Mętrak, Krzysztof. "Cztery glossy do Miłosza." *Literatura* X, no. 14(1981), pp. 7, 12.

Możejko, Edward. "Nobel prize no surprise to his fans." *Edmonton Journal,* October 18, 1980, section I, p. 14.

Pieńkosz, Konstanty. "Gdzie wschodzie słońce i kędy zapada." *Literatura* X, no. 5(1981), p. 12.

Pieszczachowicz, Jan. "Okolice Ulro." *Literatura* 12(1983), pp. 12–14.

Przybylski, Ryszard. *To jest klasycyzm.* Warsaw: Czytelnik, 1978.

Venclova, Thomas. "Poetry as Atonement." *The Polish Review* XXXI, no. 4(1986), pp. 265–71.

Volynska-Bogert, Rimma and Wojciech Zalewski. *Czesław Miłosz: An International Bibliography* 1930–1980. Ann Arbor: University of Michigan Press, 1983.

Walicki, Andrzej. *Spotkania z Miłoszem.* London: Aneks, 1985.

World Literature Today (theme issue on Czesław Miłosz) 52, no. 3 (Summer 1978), pp. 357–425.

Wyszyński, Stefan. "Do świadków promocji doktorskiej laureata nagrody Nobla Czesława Miłosza." *Kultura* 7–8(1981), p. 15.

SUBJECT INDEX

NAME INDEX

TITLE INDEX